THIS LAND IS MINE
☆ *An Anthology of American Verse*

An Anthology of AMERICAN

J. B. LIPPINCOTT COMPANY
PHILADELPHIA *and* NEW YORK

This Land is Mine

VERSE edited by Al Hine

☆ ILLUSTRATED BY Leonard Vosburgh

☆

PS
595
H5
H4

ACKNOWLEDGMENTS

Thanks go to the following publishers, agents, and individuals for their kind permission to reprint material copyrighted or controlled by them:

Brandt & Brandt for "Cotton Mather," "Captain Kidd," and "John James Audubon" by Stephen Vincent Benét, from *A Book of Americans* by Rosemary and Stephen Vincent Benét, published by Holt, Rinehart and Winston, Inc. Copyright, 1933, by Rosemary and Stephen Vincent Benét. Copyright renewed, 1961, by Rosemary Carr Benét. For a fifty-line selection from *John Brown's Body* by Stephen Vincent Benét, published by Holt, Rinehart and Winston, Inc. Copyright, 1927, 1928, by Stephen Vincent Benét. Copyright renewed, 1955, 1956, by Rosemary Carr Benét.

John Ciardi for his poem "Camptown." Copyright, 1944, 1947, by John Ciardi.

Dodd, Mead & Company for "Jesse James" from *Golden Fleece* by William Rose Benét. Copyright, 1933, 1935, by Dodd, Mead & Company.

Doubleday & Company, Inc. for "Mrs. Swartz" from *Love Sonnets of a Cave Man* by Don Marquis. Copyright, 1923, by New York Tribune, Inc.

Norma Millay Ellis for "Recuerdo" from *Collected Poems* by Edna St. Vincent Millay, published by Harper & Row. Copyright, 1922, 1950, by Edna St. Vincent Millay.

Joseph Glazer for his poem "Too Old to Work." Copyright, 1951 by Joseph Glazer.

Harcourt, Brace & World, Inc. for "next to of course god . . ." and "it's jolly . . ." from *Poems 1923-1954* by E. E. Cummings. Copyright, 1926, by Horace Liveright. Copyright, 1954 by E. E. Cummings. For "plato told him . . ." from his volume, *Poems 1923-1954* by E. E. Cummings. Copyright, 1944, by E. E. Cummings. For "Christmas Eve Under Hooker's Statue" from *Lord Weary's Castle* by Robert Lowell. Copyright, 1944, by Robert Lowell.

Contents

☆ A NEW NATION

Introduction ★ 41

☆ A NATION DIVIDED

Introduction ★ 95

☆ A NATION GROWS

Introduction ★ 125

☆ THE UNITED STATES AND A
   WORLD AT WAR

   Introduction ★ 181

INTRODUCTION

This collection grew out of two feelings, one an interest in American history, the other an affection for verse; and this an affection catholic enough to include near-doggerel as well as some lines with the magical impact of poetry. I have included poems by other than United States citizens when the work was a definite contribution to the collection.

Throughout the pages that follow you will find these two feelings united, although in putting together the book there were many times when one feeling modified or even cancelled the other. There have been many (I hope not too many) important moments in American history that have not called forth a verse response worthy of inclusion even by my generous standards. There have been other cases where I have found verses that charmed me, but which I could not stretch my conscience to include as history.

The best I can hope this book to be for a young reader is an appetizer, a stimulator of larger interest in both history and verse.

I have been using the word verse carefully and deliberately, since I want to make clear that I mean by it an inclusive collection of writing in rhyme or meter or both. Some of the items included—perhaps more than the present pernickety critical fashion might allow—seem to me to stand up as poetry, which is *of* verse but is technically and intellectually and emotionally much more. Many other items—the larger part of the book—may never lay claim to being more than verse, and some of these items may not rank high even in that category.

But these humble, occasionally mawkish and over-wrought stanzas I am willing to defend in their contexts with as much energy as for their counterparts of real po-etry.

I can defend them because they bring to this collec-tion something of the texture of their times, and this changing texture is also part of our history. In reading these verses you will find, as I found in collecting them, shifts of mood and new developments in our feelings to-ward ourselves.

I have tried, here and there, to interlard the past with later verses, although in general the selections hold true to the general spirit of their different eras in our history. One important fact about the United States is its very diversity, not simply of geography but of people, and it is this diversity of people and their opinions that has pro-tected us from complete uniformity or predictability at any period. Unpopular as well as popular opinions have usually found some way of making themselves heard, and this could be one important reason for our health and survival as a nation.

Our poets, like our historians, have traveled a long road of constant re-examination of our past and our pres-ent. Most of them have shown a stubborn refusal to deny facts, even as some new discoveries may seem to negate some old beliefs and cherished myths.

This changing temper is probably most easily seen in war verse which, since war has always been an inspirer of verse, bulks large in any historical collection. Much the same change can be seen in the war verse of England or of France, the gradual shift from almost thoughtless if stirring cheer-leading, through an occasionally cynical disillusionment, to a simpler, more personal and truer appraisal of what war means to the soldier. This is less a turning of the back on heroism than an examination of the paradox we have come to see more clearly: of heroism existing in war's frame of terror and destruction.

You may trace this yourself as you read, seeing how war verse becomes more and more concrete, more concerned with things that can be seen and felt by an individual and less with the bloodless generalities of Fame and Glory. Anyone who may view this trend negatively, as a dilution of patriotism, would do well to examine carefully the names of the writers of the selections for World War II; two-thirds of these men were in uniform when they wrote, and most of them saw combat.

I myself think and hope that this trend toward reality and concreteness can bring us to a more solid and meaningful brand of patriotism than the Fourth of July set-pieces that often twist "Our Country, right or wrong" into "Our Country is always right." Yet, for all my respect for this trend, I would not give up the bounce and energy of more youthfully American verses like *Paul Revere's Ride* or *The Battle Hymn of the Republic*.

Perhaps this combination of attitudes and this trend in verse may help you find in these pages another kind of appetizer—a stimulant to a renewed concern for *all* facets of the history of what is now, in point of continuous growth under a basic political system, one of the oldest nations in the world.

We are an interesting and rewarding nation. Not every action in our past has been fine or heroic or commendable, but the whole record is something a citizen may be proud of without frenzies of chauvinism or aggressive superiority toward the rest of the world.

Here is a very small sample of that past as an introduction to its greater richness, not only in verse but in the moving prose of endless histories.

Like any other anthology, this selection is based on the personal tastes and fancies of the person who put it together. For cuts, omissions and emphasis, I take full responsibility. The best compliment you, as a reader, can pay is to be stimulated enough to disagree and look for your own selections to fill out areas you think I may have neglected, to replace selections which you dislike either as verse or history with choices of your own.

The only use of this or any other anthology is to open doors.

THE COLONIES

FIRST THERE WERE the Indians, never quite understood, occasionally dealt with decently, usually exploited, some tribes entirely exterminated, others isolated on reservations or partially absorbed into the White Man's culture. Except for rare incidents, the story of White Man against Indian is not a pleasant one. Even in the late 1700's, Freneau felt more secure in expressing proper sentiments about dead Indians than in trying to stop the continuing pillage of Indians still alive.

The Norsemen were the first Europeans to visit the New World. They didn't stay long enough to have an Indian problem. Eric the Red and Leif Ericson almost certainly did touch on the northern American coast in the Eighth Century, but they left no verifiable traces—only a riddle for disputing historians and a heritage of Viking giants to be remembered in misty spookiness by Lanier.

The Indian Burying Ground
☆

In spite of all the learned have said,
I still my old opinion keep;
The posture, that we give the dead,
Points out the soul's eternal sleep.

Not so the ancients of these lands—
The Indian, when from life released,
Again is seated with his friends,
And shares again the joyous feast.

His imaged birds, and painted bowl,
And venison, for a journey dressed,
Bespeak the nature of the soul,
Activity, that knows no rest.

His bow, for action ready bent,
And arrow, with a head of stone,
Can only mean that life is spent,
And not the old ideas gone.

Thou, stranger, that shalt come this way,
No fraud upon the dead commit—
Observe the swelling turf, and say
They do not lie, but here they sit.

Here still a lofty rock remains,
On which the curious eye may trace
(Now wasted, half, by wearing rains)
The fancies of a ruder race.

Here still an aged elm aspires,
Beneath whose far-projecting shade

(And which the shepherd still admires)
The children of the forest played!

There oft a restless Indian queen
(Pale Shebah, with her braided hair)
And many a barbarous form is seen
To chide the man that lingers there.

By midnight moons, o'er moistening dews;
In habit for the chase arrayed,
The hunter still the deer pursues,
The hunter and the deer, a shade!

And long shall timorous fancy see
The painted chief, and pointed spear,
And Reason's self shall bow the knee
To shadows and delusions here.

PHILIP FRENEAU [1752-1832]

The Story of Vinland
☆

Far spread, below
The sea that fast hath locked in his loose flow
All secrets of Atlantis' drowned woe
Lay bound about with night on every hand,
Save down the eastern brink a shining band
Of day made out a little way from land.
Then from that shore the wind upbore a cry:
Thou Sea, thou Sea of Darkness! why,oh why
Dost waste thy West in unthrift mystery?
But ever the idiot sea-mouths foam and fill,
And never a wave doth good for man, or ill.

And Blank is king, and Nothing hath his will;
And like as grim-beaked pelicans level file
Across the sunset toward their nightly isle
On solemn wings that wave but seldomwhile,
So leanly sails the day behind the day
To where the Past's lone Rock o'erglooms the spray,
And down its mortal fissures sinks away.

Master, Master, break this ban:
The wave lacks Thee.
Oh, is it not to widen man
Stretches the sea?
Oh, must the sea-bird's idle van
Alone be free?

Into the Sea of the Dark doth creep
Bjorne's pallid sail,
As the face of a walker in his sleep,
Set rigid and most pale,
About the night doth peer and peep
In a dream of an ancient tale.

Lo, here is made a hasty cry:
Land, land, upon the west!—
God save such land! Go by, go by:
Here may no mortal rest,
Where this waste hell of slate doth lie
And grind the glacier's breast.

The sail goeth limp: he, flap and strain!
Round eastward slanteth the mast;
As the sleep-walker waked with pain,
White-clothed in the midnight blast,
Doth stare and quake, and stride again
To houseward all aghast.

. . . .

Stout Are Marson, southward whirled
From out the tempest's hand,
Doth skip the sloping of the world
To Huitramannaland,
Where Georgia's oaks with moss-beards curled
Wave by the shining strand.

. . . .

Land of large merciful-hearted skies,
Big bounties, rich increase,
Green rests for Trade's blood-shotten eyes,
For o'er-beat brains surcease,
For Love the dear woods' sympathies,
For Grief the wise woods' peace.

For Need rich givings of hid powers
In hills and vales quick-won,
For Greed large exemplary flowers
That ne'er have toiled nor spun,
For Heat fair tempered winds and showers,
For Cold the neighbor sun.

. . . .

Then Leif, bold son of Eric the Red,
To the South of the West doth flee—
Past slaty Helluland is sped,
Past Markland's woody lea,
Till round about fair Vinland's head,
Where Taunton helps the sea.

The Norseman calls, the anchor falls,
The mariners hurry a-strand:
They wassail with fore-drunken skals
Where prophet wild grapes stand;

They lift the Leifsbooth's hasty walls,
They stride about the land—

New England, thee! whose ne'er-spent wine
As blood doth stretch each vein,
And urge thee, sinewed like thy vine,
Through peril and all pain
To grasp Endeavor's towering Pine,
And, once ahold, remain—

. . . .

Now long the Sea of Darkness glimmers low
With sails from Northland flickering to and fro—
Thorwald, Karlsefne, and those twin heirs of woe,
Hellboge and Finnge, in treasonable bed
Slain by the ill-born child of Eric Red,
Freydisa false. Till, as much time is fled,
Once more the vacant airs with darkness fill,
Once more the wave doth never good nor ill,
And Blank is king, and Nothing works his will:
And leanly sails the day behind the day
To where the Past's lone Rock o'erglooms the spray,
And down its mortal fissures sinks away,
As when the grim-beaked pelicans level file
Across the sunset to their seaward isle
On solemn wings that wave but seldomwhile.

SIDNEY LANIER [1842-1881]

Vinland is an Anglicization of the alleged Norse name for the
temperate lands they discovered in North America. Eric the
Red, a Viking exile from Iceland, roved as far as the coasts of
Greenland. It was up to his son Leif to find the North American
coast and name the sections he touched: Helluland meant land
of flat rocks, Markland forest land, and Vinland wineland. Other
Norse names refer to Viking gods and heroes in the dim border-
land between historical saga and mythology.

★★★★★★★

The Spaniards made the first real landfall. Christopher Columbus was an indefinite figure in almost everything except his grim determination. He made his discovery at a time when the news could penetrate and stir a Europe at last scientifically able and commercially anxious to act upon it. Miller's verses have almost an air of self-parody now, but this should not blind us to the fact that they reflect both the monotony and the challenge of one of man's first great ventures into the unknown.

MacLeish, writing from our own day, can see the past in perspective. He sees the Spaniards' cruelty overshadowing their heroism, and leaving a memory of injustice that has never quite died away.

Columbus
☆

Behind him lay the gray Azores,
Behind the Gates of Hercules;
Before him not the ghost of shores,
Before him only shoreless seas.
The good mate said: "Now must we pray,
For lo! the very stars are gone.
Brave Admiral, speak, what shall I say?"
"Why, say 'Sail on! sail on! and on!' "

"My men grow mutinous day by day;
My men grow ghastly wan, and weak."
The stout mate thought of home; a spray
Of salt wave washed his swarthy cheek.

"What shall I say, brave Admiral, say,
If we sight naught but seas at dawn?"
"Why, you shall say at break of day,
'Sail on! sail on! sail on! and on!'"

They sailed and sailed, as winds might blow,
Until at last the blanched mate said:
"Why, now not even God would know
Should I and all my men fall dead.
These very winds forget their way,
For God from these dread seas is gone.
Now speak, brave Admiral, speak and say"—
He said: "Sail on! sail on! and on!"

They sailed. They sailed. Then spake the mate:
"This mad sea shows his teeth to-night.
He lifts his lip, he lies in wait,
With lifted teeth, as if to bite!
Brave Admiral, say but one good word:
What shall we do when hope is gone?"
The words leapt like a leaping sword:
"Sail on! sail on! sail on! and on!"

Then, pale and worn, he kept his deck,
And peered through darkness. Ah, that night
Of all dark nights! And then a speck—
A light! a light! a light! a light!
It grew to be Time's burst of dawn.
He gained a world; he gave that world
Its grandest lesson: "On! sail on!"

JOAQUIN MILLER [1839-1913]

The Fifteenth Book From
Conquistador

Conquistador . . .

☆

And we marched against them there in the next spring:
And we did the thing that time by the books and the
    science:
And we burned the back towns and we cut the mulberries:
And their dykes were down and the pipes of their
    fountains dry:

And we laid them a Christian siege with the sun and the
    vultures:
And they kept us ninety and three days till they died of it:
And the whole action well conceived and conducted:

And they cared nothing for sieges on their side:
And the place stank to God and their dung was such as
Thin swine will pass for the winter flies and the

Whole city was grubbed for the roots and their guts were
Swollen with tree-bark: and we let them go:
And they crawled out by the soiled walls and the
    rubbish—

Three days they were there on the dykes going—
And the captains ill of the bad smell of that city
And the town gone—no stone to a stone of it—

And the whole thing was a very beautiful victory:
And we squared the streets like a city in old Spain
And we built barracks and shops: and the church
    conspicuous:

And those that had jeered at our youth (but the fashion
    changes:)
They came like nettles in dry slash: like beetles:
They ran on the new land like lice staining it:

They parcelled the bloody meadows: their late feet
Stood in the passes of harsh pain and of winter:
In the stale of the campments they culled herbs: they
    peeled the

Twigs of the birch and they stood at the hill-fights
    thinking:
They brought carts with their oak beds and their boards
    and the
Pots they had and the stale clothes and the stink of

Stewed grease in the gear and their wives before them
Sour and smelling of spent milk and their children:
They built their barns like the old cotes under Cordova:

They raised the Spanish cities: the new hills
Showed as the old with the old walls and the tether of
Galled goats in the dung and the rock hidden . . .

Old . . . an old man sickened and near death:

And the west is gone now: the west is the ocean sky . . .
O day that brings the earth back bring again

That well-swept town those towers and that island. . . .

ARCHIBALD MACLEISH [1892-   ]

★★★★★★★

England saw the new lands as romance and excitement
and riches and adventure. Marvell and Drayton cele-
brated the New World in the elegant imagery of my-
thology.

The early British colony at Jamestown hacked out an
enduring claim for its namesake king. It was also the
scene of the love story of Captain John Smith and Poca-
hantas (she later *was* wedded to an Englishman, not
Smith but John Rolfe) a mixture of legend and history.

Farther north, the Massachusetts settlers were not at
all in the mood to name their colony for a king whose re-
ligious restrictions they had fled. They owed nominal
allegiance to England, but the respects they first paid
were to their stern and upright Puritan God.

Bermudas
☆

Where the remote Bermudas ride
In the ocean's bosom unespied,
From a small boat, that rowed along,
The listening winds received this song:

"What should we do but sing His praise,
That led us through the watery maze,
Unto an isle so long unknown,
And yet far kinder than our own?
Where He the huge sea-monsters wracks,
That lift the deep upon their backs,
He lands us on a grassy stage,
Safe from the storms, and prelates' rage.
He gave us this eternal Spring
Which here enamels every thing,
And sends the fowls to us in care,
On daily visits through the air;
He hangs in shades the orange bright,
Like golden lamps in a green night,
And does in the pomegranates close
Jewels more rich than Ormus shows;
He makes the figs our mouths to meet,
And throws the melons at our feet;
But apples plants of such a price,
No tree could ever bear them twice.
With cedars chosen by His hand
From Lebanon He stores the land,
And makes the hollow seas that roar
Proclaim the ambergris on shore;
He cast (of which we rather boast)
The Gospel's pearl upon our coast,
And in these rocks for us did frame
A temple where to sound His name.
Oh! let our voice His praise exalt,
Till it arrive at Heaven's vault,
Which thence (perhaps) rebounding may
Echo beyond the Mexique Bay."

Thus sung they, in the English boat,
A holy and a cheerful note:

And all the way, to guide their chime,
With falling oars they kept the time.

ANDREW MARVELL [1621-1678]

To the Virginian Voyage
☆

You brave heroic minds,
Worthy your country's name,
That honor still pursue,
Go and subdue,
Whilst loitering hinds
Lurk here at home, with shame.

Britons, you stay too long:
Quickly aboard bestow you,
And with a merry gale
Swell your stretch'd sail,
With vows as strong
As the winds that blow you.

Your course securely steer,
West and by south forth keep!
Rocks, lee-shores, nor shoals,
When Eolus scowls,
You need not fear,
So absolute the deep.

And cheerfully at sea,
Success you still entice,
To get the pearl and gold,
And ours to hold
Virginia,
Earth's only paradise.

Where nature hath in store
Fowl, venison, and fish,
And the fruitful'st soil,
Without your toil,
Three harvests more,
All greater than your wish.

And the ambitious vine
Crowns with his purple mass
The cedar reaching high
To kiss the sky,
The cypress, pine,
And useful sassafras.

To whom the Golden Age
Still nature's laws doth give,
No other cares attend,
But them to defend
From winter's rage,
That long there doth not live.

When as the luscious smell
Of that delicious land,
Above the seas that flows,
The clear wind throws,
Your hearts to swell
Approaching the dear strand;

In kenning of the shore
(Thanks to God first given)
O you the happiest men,
Be frolic then!
Let cannons roar,
Frighting the wide heaven;

And in regions far
Such heroes bring ye forth
As those from whom we came,
And plant our name
Under that star
Not known unto our North;

And as there plenty grows
Of laurel everywhere,—
Apollo's sacred tree,—
You it may see,
A poet's brows
To crown, that may sing there.

The Voyages attend
Industrious Hackluit,
Whose reading shall inflame
Men to seek fame,
And much commend
To after-times thy wit.

MICHAEL DRAYTON [1563-1631]

Pocahontas

☆

Wearied arm, and broken sword
Wage in vain the desperate fight;
Round him press a countless horde,
He is but a single knight.
Hark! a cry of triumph shrill
Through the wilderness resounds,
As, with twenty bleeding wounds,
Sinks the warrior, fighting still.

Now they heap the funeral pyre,
And the torch of death they light;
Ah! 'tis hard to die by fire!
Who will shield the captive knight?
Round the stake with fiendish cry
Wheel and dance the savage crowd,
Cold the victim's mien and proud,
And his breast is bared to die.

Who will shield the fearless heart?
Who avert the murderous blade?
From the throng with sudden start
See, there springs an Indian maid.
Quick she stands before the knight:
"Loose the chain, unbind the ring!
I am daughter of the king,
And I claim the Indian right!"

Dauntlessly aside she flings
Lifted axe and thirsty knife,
Fondly to his heart she clings,
And her bosom guards his life!
In the woods of Powhatan
Still 'tis told by Indian fires
How a daughter of their sires
Saved a captive Englishman.

WILLIAM MAKEPEACE THACKERAY [1811-1863]

Landing of the Pilgrim Fathers
☆

The breaking waves dashed high
On the stern and rock-bound coast,
And the woods, against a stormy sky,
Their giant branches tossed;

And the heavy night hung dark
The hills and waters o'er,
When a band of exiles moored their bark
On the wild New England shore.

Not as the conqueror comes,
They, the true-hearted, came:
Not with the roll of the stirring drums,
And the trumpet that sings of fame;

Not as the flying come,
In silence and in fear,—
They shook the depths of the desert's gloom
With their hymns of lofty cheer.

Amidst the storm they sang,
And the stars heard, and the sea;

And the sounding aisles of the dim woods rang
To the anthem of the free!

The ocean-eagle soared
From his nest by the white wave's foam,
And the rocking pines of the forest roared:
This was their welcome home!

There were men with hoary hair
Amidst that pilgrim band;
Why have they come to winter there,
Away from their childhood's land?

There was woman's fearless eye,
Lit by her deep love's truth;
There was manhood's brow, serenely high,
And the fiery heart of youth.

What sought they thus afar?
Bright jewels of the mine?
The wealth of seas, the spoils of war?—
They sought a faith's pure shrine!

Aye, call it holy ground,
The soil where first they trod!
They have left unstained what there they found—
Freedom to worship God!

FELICIA HEMANS [1793-1835]

The First Thanksgiving Day
☆

"And now," said the Governor, gazing abroad on the
     piled-up store
Of the sheaves that dotted the clearings and covered the
     meadows o'er,

" 'Tis meet that we render praises because of this yield of
   grain;
'Tis meet that the Lord of the harvest be thanked for His
   sun and rain.

"And therefore, I, William Bradford (by the grace of God
   to-day,
And the franchise of this good people), Governor of
   Plymouth, say,
Through virtue of vested power—ye shall gather with one
   accord,
And hold, in the month November, thanksgiving unto the
   Lord.

"He hath granted us peace and plenty, and the quiet we've
   sought so long;
He hath thwarted the wily savage, and kept him from
   wrack and wrong;
And unto our feast the Sachem shall be bidden, that he
   may know
We worship his own Great Spirit who maketh the harvests
   grow.

"So shoulder your matchlocks, masters: there is hunting of
   all degrees;
And fishermen, take you tackle, and scour for spoil the
   seas;
And maidens and dames of Plymouth, your delicate crafts
   employ
To honor our First Thanksgiving, and make it a feast of
   joy!

"We fail of the fruits and dainties—we fail of the old home
   cheer;
Ah, these are the lightest losses, mayhap, that befall us
   here;

But see in our open clearings, how golden the melons lie;
Enrich them with sweets and spices, and give us the
    pumpkin-pie!"

So, bravely the preparations went on for the autumn feast;
The deer and the bear were slaughtered; wild game from
    the greatest to least
Was heaped in the colony cabins; brown home-brew served
    for wine,
And the plum and the grape of the forest, for orange and
    peach and pine.

MARGARET JUNKIN PRESTON [1820-1897]

★★★★★★★

It was a hard life and an exciting one in the Colonies.
Above all it was uncertain. One day William Kidd might
be just another reckless seaman, raiding French merchant
ships with the blessings of His Britannic Majesty; the
next day Captain Kidd, the Pirate, would hang in chains
for carrying his raiding too far.

One day the wife next door might be another friendly
matron; the next day—hysteria spread by gossip, the
grim theology of a Cotton Mather turning a religion of
love inside-out—she might stand trembling in court as
an accused witch.

Captain Kidd
1650-1701
☆

This person in the gaudy clothes
Is worthy Captain Kidd.
They say he never buried gold,
I think, perhaps, he did.

They say it's all a story that
His favorite little song
Was "Make these lubbers walk the plank!"
I think, perhaps, they're wrong.

They say he never pirated
Beneath the Skull-and-Bones.
He merely traveled for his health
And spoke in soothing tones.

In fact, you'll read in nearly all
The newer history books
That he was mild as cottage cheese
—But I don't like his looks!

STEPHEN VINCENT BENÉT [1898-1943]

Giles Corey
☆

Giles Corey was a Wizzard strong,
A stubborn wretch was he;
And fitt was he to hang on high
Upon the Locust-tree.

So when before the magistrates
For trial he did come,
He would no true confession make,
But was compleatlie dumbe.

"Giles Corey," said the Magistrate,
"What hast thou heare to pleade
To these that now accuse thy soule
Of crimes and horrid deed?"

Giles Corey, he said not a worde,
No single worde spoke he.
"Giles Corey," saith the Magistrate,
"We'll press it out of thee."

They got them then a heavy beam,
They laid it on his breast;
They loaded it with heavy stones,
And hard upon him prest.

"More weight!" now said this wretched man;
"More weight!" again he cried;
And he did no confession make,
But wickedly he dyed.

ANONYMOUS

Cotton Mather
1663-1728
☆

Grim Cotton Mather
Was always seeing witches,
Daylight, moonlight,

They buzzed about his head,
Pinching him and plaguing him
With aches and pains and stitches,
Witches in his pulpit,
Witches by his bed.

Nowadays, nowadays,
We'd say that he was crazy,
But everyone believed him
In old Salem town
And nineteen people
Were hanged for Salem witches
Because of Cotton Mather
And his long, black gown.

Old Cotton Mather
Didn't die happy.
He could preach and thunder,
He could fast and pray,
But men began to wonder
If there had been witches—
When he walked in the streets
Men looked the other way.

STEPHEN VINCENT BENÉT [1898-1943]

★★★★★★★

Soon there were the French to worry about as well as
the Indians and witches. Sometimes Frenchmen and In-
dians warred together against the British; sometimes
there were Indians on both sides trying to preserve what

they could of their own ancestral lands. Braddock's British force was wiped out as it marched on Fort Duquesne; but four years later George Washington, the young Virginian who had accompanied Braddock, came back with General James Forbes to defeat the French. He renamed their stockade Fort Pitt in honor of the British minister who had put new vigor into the war.

Only a few months earlier, British generals Jeffrey Amherst and James Wolfe had led the successful campaign to recapture the French fort at Louisburg in Nova Scotia. The following year (1759) saw the end of French power in Canada. Wolfe defeated Montcalm on the Plains of Abraham below Quebec, dying in battle, but not before he knew his victory was secure.

Louisburg
☆

Neptune and Mars in Council sate
To humble France's pride,
Whose vain unbridled insolence
All other Powers defied.

The gods having sat in deep debate
Upon the puzzling theme,
Broke up perplexed and both agreed
Shirley should form the scheme.

Shirley, with Britain's glory fired,
Heaven's favoring smile implored:
"Let Louisburg return,"—he said,
"Unto its ancient Lord."

At once the Camp and Fleet were filled
With Britain's loyal sons,
Whose hearts are filled with generous strife
T'avenge their Country's wrongs.

With Liberty their breasts are filled,
Fair Liberty's their shield;
'Tis Liberty their banner waves
And hovers o'er their field.

Louis!—behold the unequal strife,
Thy slaves in walls immured!
While George's sons laugh at those walls—
Of victory assured.

One key to your oppressive pride
Your Western Dunkirk's gone;
So Pepperell and Warren bade
And what they bade was done!

Forbear, proud Prince, your gasconades,
Te Deums cease to sing,—
When Britains fight the Grand Monarque
Must yield to Britain's King.

ANONYMOUS

Louis was Louis XV of France, the Grand Monarque. George, of
course, was George II, King of England including the American
Colonies.

Shirley was Sir William Shirley, governor of Massachusetts,
who planned the 1745 campaign against Louisburg. Sir William
Pepperell was the general and Sir Peter Warren the naval officer
who carried out the successful action. Pepperell, as reward for
this victory, became the first Colonial to be granted a baronetcy.

The French retook Louisburg in 1748, but it fell again and
finally to British-Colonial forces led by Lord Jeffrey Amherst in
1758.

The reference to "Western Dunkirk" compares the fortress of Louisburg to the famous French stronghold on the Belgian border.

Braddock's Fate, with an Incitement to Revenge
☆

Come all ye sons of Brittany,
Assist my muse in tragedy,
And mourn brave Braddock's destiny,
And spend a mournful day,
Upon Monongahela fields,
The mighty're fallen o'er their shields;
And British blood bedews the hills
Of western Gilboa.

July the ninth, oh! Fatal Day,
They had a bold and bloody fray,
Our host was smote with a dismay;
Some basely did retire,
And left brave Braddock in the field,
Who had much rather die than yield,
A while his sword he bravely wield
In clouds of smoke and fire.

Some time he bravely stood his ground,
A thousand foes did him surround,
Till he received a mortal wound,
Which forc'd him to retreat.
He dy'd upon the thirteenth day,
As he was home-ward on his way;
Alas! alas! we all must say,
A sore and sad defeat.

Now to his grave this hero's borne,
While savage foes triumph and scorn,
And drooping banners dress his urn,
And guard him to his tomb.
Heralds and monarchs of the dead,
You that so many worms have fed,
He's coming to your chilly bed,
Edge close and give him room.

HIS EPITAPH

Beneath this stone brave Braddock lies,
Who always hated cowardice,
But fell a savage sacrifice
Amidst his Indian foes.
I charge you, heroes, of the ground,
To guard his dark pavilion round,
And keep off all obtruding sound,
And cherish his repose.

. . . .

A SURVEY OF THE FIELD OF BATTLE

Return my muse unto the field,
See what a prospect it doth yield;

Ingrateful to the eyes and smell
A carnage bath'd in gore,
Lies scalp'd and mangled o'er the hills,
While sanguine rivers fill the dales,
And pale-fac'd horror spreads the fields,
The like ne'er here before.

. . . .

Revenge, revenge the harmless blood
Which their inhuman dogs have shed
In every frontier neighborhood,
For near these hundred years.
Their murdering clan in ambush lies,
To kill and scalp them by surprise,
And free from tender parents' eyes
Ten hundred thousand tears.

. . . .

One bold effort, oh, let us make,
And at one blow behead the snake,
And then these savage powers will break,
Which long have us oppress'd.
And this, brave soldiers, will we do
If Heaven and George shall say so too;
And if we drive the matter thro',
The land will be at rest.

. . . .

O mother land, we think we're sure,
Sufficient is thy marine powers
To dissipate all eastern showers:
And if our arms be blest,

Thy sons in North America
Will drive these hell-born dogs away
As far beyond the realms of day,
As east is from the west.

Forbear my muse thy barbarous song,
Upon this theme thou'st dwelt too long,
It is too high and much too strong,
The learned won't allow.
Much honor should accrue to him
Who ne'er was at their Academ
Come blot out every telesem;
Get home unto thy plow.

STEPHEN TILDEN [1686-1766]

Brave Wolfe
☆

Cheer up, ye young men all, let nothing fright you;
Though at your love's pursuits, let that delight you;
Don't let your fancy move when come to trial,
Nor let your courage fail at the first denial.

"Bad news has come to town, bad news has carried;
Bad news is whispered round—my love is married.
I'll away to the wars of France where cannon rattle,
Myself I will advance in the front of battle.

"I would go tell my love I'm going to leave her,
Down to the wars of France I'm bound forever;
But whene'er I go to speak, my tongue doth quiver,
So I dare not tell my mind when I am with her.

"Here is a ring of gold, if you'll accept it;
Here, here is a ring of gold, long time I've kept it.
Whene'er you the posy read, think of the giver.
Madam, remember me; I'm done forever."

So then this gallant youth took to the ocean
To free America from its commotion.
We landed at Quebec with all our party,
The city to attack, being brave and hearty.

Brave Wolfe and Montcalm like brothers talked,
And lovingly between their armies walked,
Till each one took his post as they retired;
Brave Wolfe took his leave and for death prepared.

Till each one took his post as they retired.
So then this numerous host began their fire,
When shot down from his horse fell this brave hero
We do lament his loss in words of sorrow.

He lifted up his head as he lay dying;
The French their ranks had broke, and the troops
        were flying.
He lifted up his head while the drum did rattle,
And to his army said, "How goes the battle?"

His aide-de-camp replied: "All in our favor.
Quebec will fall a prize, nothing can save her;
She'll fall into our hands with all her treasure."
So then replies brave Wolfe, "I die with pleasure."

ANONYMOUS

A NEW NATION

THE AMERICAN REVOLUTION was slow in starting and long in coming to the end we like to think was predestined. Its first stirrings grew more from petty irritations than from the high ideals that were formulated later. Annoying taxes, lack of understanding in England, the arrogance of some British governors and officers, all piled up into an intolerable burden. Yet at the beginning the fieriest rebels asked only for Colonial representation in the British Parliament that governed them. It was not until conflict became a reality that the Adams brothers, along with Monroe, Madison, Jefferson and Franklin, formulated the idea of a new and free nation. These men and some others who worked with them made up one of the finest combinations of political intelligences ever gathered together.

The famous Tea Party, at which proper Bostonians masqueraded as Indians to dump tea in the harbor rather than pay the Crown Tax, was not held until 1773. The First Continental Congress, a body bent still on conciliation with Britain, met in Philadelphia in September of 1774. But events were moving too swiftly for conciliation. In April of 1775, when fresh British troops were landed, Paul Revere and the less celebrated William

Dawes spread the word on horseback. The first shots of real Revolution were fired at Concord on April 19.

It was a long, see-saw struggle. British troops and Tory sympathizers held strong positions along the whole sea-board and there were periods when Independence seemed a lost cause. Nathan Hale was hanged as a spy by the British in New York in 1776. Molly Pitcher (Mary Ludwig Hays McCauley) manned her husband's cannon at the battle of Monmouth, New Jersey, in 1778 and won lasting fame.

In the south, the British defeated Greene at Eutaw Springs, but were never able to subdue the guerrilla raiders of General Francis Marion, the Swamp Fox. When an end came with peace in 1783, our independence from Great Britain was an accepted fact. There were, however, still six more years of thoughtful consultation in the thirteen colonies before a central government could be agreed upon. When this came into being, there was unanimous agreement in the choice of General George Washington as first president in 1789.

A Ballad of the Boston Tea-Party
☆

No! never such a draught was poured
Since Hebe served with nectar
The bright Olympians and their Lord,
Her over-kind protector,—

Since Father Noah squeezed the grape
And took to such behaving

As would have shamed our grandsire ape
Before the days of shaving,—

No! ne'er was mingled such a draught
In palace, hall, or arbor,
As freemen brewed and tyrants quaffed
That night in Boston Harbor!

It kept King George so long awake
His brain at last got addled,
It made the nerves of Britain shake,
With sevenscore millions saddled;

Before that bitter cup was drained
Amid the roar of cannon,
The Western war-cloud's crimson stained
The Thames, the Clyde, the Shannon;

Full many a six-foot grenadier
The flattened grass had measured,
And many a mother many a year
Her tearful memories treasured;

Fast spread the tempest's darkening pall,
The mighty realms were troubled,
The storm broke loose, but first of all
The Boston teapot bubbled!

An evening party,—only that,
No formal invitation,
No gold-laced coat, no stiff cravat,
No feast in contemplation,

No silk-robed dames, no fiddling band,
No flowers, no songs, no dancing,—

A tribe of red men, axe in hand,—
Behold the guests advancing!

How fast the stragglers join the throng,
From stall and workshop gathered!
The lively barber skips along
And leaves a chin half-lathered;

The smith has flung his hammer down,—
The horseshoe still is glowing;
The truant tapster at the Crown
Has left a beer-cask flowing;

The cooper's boys have dropped the adze,
And trot behind their master;
Up run the tarry ship-yard lads,—
The crowd is hurrying faster,—

Out from the Millpond's purlieus gush
The streams of white-faced millers,
And down their slippery alleys rush
The lusty young Fort-Hillers;

The ropewalk lends its 'prentice crew,—
The tories seize the omen:
"Ay, boys, you'll soon have work to do
For England's rebel foemen,

'King Hancock,' Adams, and their gang,
That fire the mob with treason,—
When these we shoot and those we hang
The town will come to reason."

On—on to where the tea-ships ride!
And now their ranks are forming,—
A rush, and up the *Dartmouth's* side
The Mohawk band is swarming!

See the fierce natives! What a glimpse
Of paint and fur and feather,
As all at once the full-grown imps
Light on the deck together!

A scarf the pigtail's secret keeps,
A blanket hides the breeches,—
And out the cursèd cargo leaps,
And overboard it pitches!

O woman, at the evening board
So gracious, sweet, and purring,
So happy while the tea is poured,
So blest while spoons are stirring,

What martyr can compare with thee,
The mother, wife, or daughter,
That night, instead of best Bohea,
Condemned to milk and water!

Ah, little dreams the quiet dame
Who plies with rock and spindle
The patient flax, how great a flame
Yon little spark shall kindle!

The lurid morning shall reveal
A fire no king can smother
Where British flint and Boston steel
Have clashed against each other!

Old charters shrivel in its track,
His Worship's bench has crumbled,
It climbs and clasps the Union-Jack,
Its blazoned pomp is humbled,

The flags go down on land and sea
Like corn before the reapers;
So burned the fire that brewed the tea
That Boston served her keepers!

The waves that wrought a century's wreck
Have rolled o'er whig and tory;
The Mohawks on the *Dartmouth*'s deck
Still live in song and story;

The waters in the rebel bay
Have kept the tea-leaf savor;
Our old North-Enders in their spray
Still taste a Hyson flavor;

And Freedom's teacup still o'erflows
With ever fresh libations,
To cheat of slumber all her foes
And cheer the wakening nations!

OLIVER WENDELL HOLMES [1809-1894]

Hebe, in Greek mythology, was cup-bearer to the gods although
one may doubt that she ever served them tea. King Hancock was
John Hancock, later to sign the boldest signature on the Declara-
tion of Independence, and Adams was Samuel Adams of the clan
that gave us two presidents, John and John Quincy. Hyson is a
type of green tea from China.

Paul Revere's Ride

☆

Listen, my children, and you shall hear
Of the midnight ride of Paul Revere,
On the eighteenth of April, in Seventy-five;
Hardly a man is now alive
Who remembers that famous day and year.

He said to his friend, "If the British march
By land or sea from the town to-night,
Hang a lantern aloft in the belfry arch
Of the North Church tower as a signal light,—
One, if by land, and two, if by sea;
And I on the opposite shore will be,
Ready to ride and spread the alarm
Through every Middlesex village and farm,
For the country folk to be up and to arm."

Then he said, "Good night!" and with muffled oar
Silently rowed to the Charlestown shore,
Just as the moon rose over the bay,
Where swinging wide at her moorings lay
The Somerset, British man-of-war;
A phantom ship, with each mast and spar
Across the moon like a prison bar,
And a huge black hulk, that was magnified
By its own reflection in the tide.

Meanwhile, his friend, through alley and street,
Wanders and watches with eager ears,
Till in the silence around him he hears
The muster of men at the barrack door,
The sound of arms, and the tramp of feet,
And the measured tread of the grenadiers,
Marching down to their boats on the shore.

Then he climbed the tower of the Old North Church,
By the wooden stairs, with stealthy tread,
To the belfry-chamber overhead,
And startled the pigeons from their perch
On the sombre rafters, that round him made
Masses and moving shapes of shade,—
By the trembling ladder, steep and tall,
To the highest window in the wall,
Where he paused to listen and look down
A moment on the roofs of the town,
And the moonlight flowing over all.

Beneath, in the churchyard, lay the dead,
In their night-encampment on the hill,
Wrapped in silence so deep and still
That he could hear, like a sentinel's tread,
The watchful night-wind, as it went
Creeping along from tent to tent,
And seeming to whisper, "All is well!"
A moment only he feels the spell
Of the place and the hour, and the secret dread
Of the lonely belfry and the dead;
For suddenly all his thoughts are bent
On a shadowy something far away,
Where the river widens to meet the bay,—
A line of black that bends and floats
On the rising tide, like a bridge of boats.

Meanwhile, impatient to mount and ride,
Booted and spurred, with a heavy stride
On the opposite shore walked Paul Revere.
Now he patted his horse's side,
Now gazed at the landscape far and near,
Then, impetuous, stamped the earth,
And turned and tightened his saddle girth;

But mostly he watched with eager search
The belfry-tower of the Old North Church,
Lonely and spectral and sombre and still.
And lo! as he looks, on the belfry's height
A glimmer, and then a gleam of light!
He springs to the saddle, the bridle he turns,
But lingers and gazes, till full on his sight
A second lamp in the belfry burns!

A hurry of hoofs in a village street,
A shape in the moonlight, a bulk in the dark,
And beneath, from the pebbles, in passing, a spark
Struck out by a steed flying fearless and fleet:
That was all! And yet, through the gloom and the
    light,
The fate of a nation was riding that night;
And the spark struck out by that steed, in his flight,
Kindled the land into flame with its heat.

He has left the village and mounted the steep,
And beneath him, tranquil and broad and deep,
Is the Mystic, meeting the ocean tides;
And under the alders that skirt its edge,
Now soft on the sand, now loud on the ledge,
Is heard the tramp of his steed as he rides.

It was twelve by the village clock,
When he crossed the bridge into Medford town.
He heard the crowing of the cock,
And the barking of the farmer's dog,
And felt the damp of the river fog,
That rises after the sun goes down.

It was one by the village clock,
When he galloped into Lexington.
He saw the gilded weathercock

Swing in the moonlight as he passed,
And the meeting-house windows, blank and bare,
Gaze at him with a spectral glare,
As if they already stood aghast
At the bloody work they would look upon.

It was two by the village clock,
When he came to the bridge in Concord town.
He heard the bleating of the flock,
And the twitter of birds among the trees,
And felt the breath of the morning breeze
Blowing over the meadows brown.
And one was safe and asleep in his bed
Who at the bridge would be first to fall,
Who that day would be lying dead,
Pierced by a British musket-ball.

You know the rest. In the books you have read,
How the British Regulars fired and fled,—
How the farmers gave them ball for ball,
From behind each fence and farm-yard wall,
Chasing the red-coats down the land,
Then crossing the fields to emerge again
Under the trees at the turn of the road,
And only pausing to fire and load.

So through the night rode Paul Revere;
And so through the night went his cry of alarm
To every Middlesex village and farm,—
A cry of defiance and not of fear,
A voice in the darkness, a knock at the door,
And a word that shall echo forevermore!
For, borne on the night-wind of the Past,
Through all our history, to the last,
In the hour of darkness and peril and need,
The people will waken and listen to hear
The hurrying hoof-beats of that steed,
And the midnight message of Paul Revere.

HENRY WADSWORTH LONGFELLOW [1807-1882]

Concord Hymn
☆

By the rude bridge that arched the flood,
Their flag to April's breeze unfurled,
Here once the embattled farmers stood,
And fired the shot heard round the world.

The foe long since in silence slept;
Alike the conqueror silent sleeps;

And Time the ruined bridge has swept
Down the dark stream which seaward creeps.

On this green bank, by this soft stream,
We set to-day a votive stone;
That memory may their deed redeem,
When, like our sires, our sons are gone.

Spirit that made those heroes dare
To die, and leave their children free,
Bid Time and Nature gently spare
The shaft we raise to them and thee.

RALPH WALDO EMERSON [1803-1882]

Nathan Hale
☆

To drum-beat and heart-beat,
A soldier marches by;
There is color in his cheek,
There is courage in his eye,
Yet to the drum-beat and heart-beat
In a moment he must die.

By starlight and moonlight,
He seeks the Briton's camp;
He hears the rustling flag
And the armed sentry's tramp;
And the starlight and moonlight
His silent wandering's lamp.

With slow tread and still tread,
He scans the tented line;

And he counts the battery guns,
By the gaunt and shadowy pine;
And his slow tread and still tread
Gives no warning sign.

The dark wave, the plumed wave,
It meets his eager glance;
And it sparkles 'neath the stars,
Like the glimmer of a lance—
A dark wave, a plumed wave,
On an emerald expanse.

A sharp clang, a still clang,
And terror in the sound!
For the sentry, falcon-eyed,
In the camp a spy hath found;
With a sharp clang, a steel clang,
The patriot is bound.

With calm brow, and steady brow,
He listens to his doom;
In his look there is no fear,
Nor a shadow-trace of gloom;
But with calm brow and steady brow,
He robes him for the tomb.

In the long night, the still night,
He kneels upon the sod;
And the brutal guards withhold
E'en the solemn word of God!
In the long night, the still night,
He walks where Christ hath trod.

'Neath the blue morn, the sunny morn,
He dies upon the tree;

And he mourns that he can lose
But one life for Liberty;
And in the blue morn, the sunny morn,
His spirit wings are free.

But his last words, his message-words,
They burn, lest friendly eye
Should read how proud and calm
A patriot could die,
With his last words, his dying words,
A soldier's battle-cry.

From Fame-leaf and Angel-leaf,
From monument and urn,
The sad of earth, the glad of heaven,
His tragic fate shall learn;
But on Fame-leaf and Angel-leaf
The name of HALE shall burn!

FRANCIS MILES FINCH [1827-1907]

Molly Pitcher
☆

All day the great guns barked and roared;
All day the big balls screeched and soared;
All day, 'mid the sweating gunners grim,
Who toiled in their smoke-shroud dense and dim,
Sweet Molly labored with courage high,
With steady hand and watchful eye,
Till the day was ours, and the sinking sun
Looked down on the field of Monmouth won,
And Molly standing beside her gun.

Now, Molly, rest your weary arm!
Safe, Molly, all is safe from harm.
Now, woman, bow your aching head,
And weep in sorrow o'er your dead!

Next day on that field so hardly won,
Stately and calm stands Washington,
And looks where our gallant Greene doth lead
A figure clad in motley weed—
A soldier's cap and a soldier's coat
Masking a woman's petticoat.
He greets our Molly in kindly wise;
He bids her raise her tearful eyes;
And now he hails her before them all
Comrade and soldier, whate'er befall,
"And since she has played a man's full part,
A man's reward for her loyal heart!
And Sergeant Molly Pitcher's name
Be writ henceforth on the shield of fame!"

Oh, Molly, with your eyes so blue!
Oh, Molly, Molly, here's to you!
Sweet honor's roll will aye be richer
To hold the name of Molly Pitcher.

LAURA E. RICHARDS [1850-1943]

Molly Pitcher was born Mary Ludwig. At the time of the Battle
of Monmouth she was married to John Caspar Hays, an artillery-
man. She won the "Pitcher" nickname by serving drafts of cold
water to thirsty soldiers and her lasting fame, as in the poem, by
taking over her husband's gun when he collapsed from heat and
exhaustion. She remarried after Hays's death in 1789 and lived
as Mary Ludwig Hays McCauley to the ripe old age, for that
era, of 68. In 1822 the Pennsylvania Assembly voted an annuity
for "Molly M'Kolly" in memory of her Monmouth heroism.

Song of Marion's Men

☆

Our band is few, but true and tried,
Our leader frank and bold;
The British soldier trembles
When Marion's name is told,
Our fortress is the good greenwood,
Our tent the cypress-tree;
We know the forest round us
As seamen know the sea.
We know its walls of thorny vines,
Its glades of reedy grass,
Its safe and silent islands
Within the dark morass.

Woe to the English soldiery
That little dread us near!

On them shall light at midnight
A strange and sudden fear:
When, waking to their tents on fire,
They grasp their arms in vain,
And they who stand to face us
Are beat to earth again;
And they who fly in terror deem
A mighty host behind,
And hear the tramp of thousands
Upon the hollow wind.

Then sweet the hour that brings release
From danger and from toil;
We talk the battle over,
We share the battle's spoil.
The woodland rings with laugh and shout,
As if a hunt were up,
And woodland flowers are gathered
To crown the soldier's cup.
With merry songs we mock the wind
That in the pine-top grieves,
And slumber long and sweetly
On beds of oaken leaves.

Well knows the fair and friendly moon
The band that Marion leads—
The glitter of their rifles,
The scampering of their steeds.
'Tis life to guide the fiery barb
Across the moonlight plain;
'Tis life to feel the night-wind
That lifts his tossing mane.
A moment in the British camp—
A moment—and away,
Back to the pathless forest
Before the peep of day.

Grave men there are by broad Santee,
Grave men with hoary hairs;
Their hearts are all with Marion,
For Marion are their prayers.
And lovely ladies greet our band
With kindliest welcoming,
With smiles like those of summer,
And tears like those of spring,
For them we wear these trusty arms,
And lay them down no more
Till we have driven the Briton
Forever from our shore.

WILLIAM CULLEN BRYANT [1794-1878]

★★★★★★★

The new republic was launched, and the men who launched it grew old, died and became distant figures in its hall of fame. Benjamin Franklin died in 1790, just as the United States had come into being.

The new nation had growing pains. Aaron Burr, then considered one of its most brilliant patriots, was vice-president under Jefferson. Burr dreamed of unlimited expansion to the west, including the seizure of Mexico. It has never been entirely clear (despite the cocksure tone of Read's verse) whether Burr wanted the land for addition to the United States or for an empire of his own. A court acquitted him of treason, but he left the United States to live out his remaining years in self-exile in England.

On the Death of Benjamin Franklin
☆

Thus, some tall tree that long hath stood
The glory of its native wood,
By storms destroyed, or length of years,
Demands the tribute of our tears.

The pile, that took long time to raise,
To dust returns by slow decays;
But when its destined years are o'er,
We must regret the loss the more.

So long accustomed to your aid,
The world laments your exit made;
So long befriended by your art,
Philosopher, 'tis hard to part!—

When monarchs tumble to the ground
Successors easily are found;
But, matchless Franklin! what a few
Can hope to rival such as you,
Who seized from kings their sceptred pride,
And turned the lightning's darts aside!

PHILIP FRENEAU [1752-1832]

Blennerhassett's Island
☆

Once came an exile, longing to be free,
Born in the greenest island of the sea;
He sought out this, the fairest blooming isle

That ever gemmed a river; and its smile,
Of summer green and freedom, on his heart
Fell, like the light of Paradise. Apart
It lay, remote and wild; and in his breast
He fancied this an island of the blest;
And here he deemed the world might never mar
The tranquil air with its molesting jar. . . .
And here he brought his household; here his wife,
As happy as her children, round his life
Sang as she were an echo, or a part
Of the deep pleasure springing in his heart—
A silken string which with the heavier cord
Made music, such as well-strung harps afford.
She was the embodied spirit of the man,
His second self, but on a fairer plan.
And here they came, and here they built their home,
And set the rose and taught the vines to roam,
Until the place became an isle of bowers,
Where odors, mist-like, swam above the flowers. . . .
It was, in sooth, a fair enchanted isle,
Round which the unbroken forest, many a mile,
Reached the horizon like a boundless sea;—
A sea whose waves, at last, were forced to flee
On either hand, before the westward host,
To meet no more upon its ancient coast
But all things fair, save truth, are frail and doomed;
And brightest beauty is the first consumed
By envious Time; as if he crowned the brow
With loveliest flowers, before he gave the blow
Which laid the victim on the hungry shrine:—
Such was the dreamer's fate, and such, bright isle,
    was thine.
There came the stranger, heralded by fame,
Whose eloquent soul was like a tongue of flame,
Which brightened and despoiled whate'er it touched.

A violet, by an iron gauntlet clutched,
Were not more doomed than whosoe'er he won
To list his plans, with glowing words o'errun:
And Blennerhassett hearkened as he planned.
Far in the South there was a glorious land
Crowned with perpetual flowers, and where repute
Pictured the gold more plenteous than the fruit—
The Persia of the West. There would he steer
His conquering course; and o'er the bright land rear
His far-usurping banner, till his home
Should rest beneath a wide, imperial dome,
Where License, round his thronèd feet, should whirl
Her dizzy mazes like an Orient girl.
His followers should be lords; their ladies each
Wear wreaths of gems beyond the old world's reach;
And emperors, gazing to that land of bloom,
With impotent fire of envy should consume.
Such was the gorgeous vision which he drew.
The listener saw; and dazzled by the view,—
As one in some enchanter's misty room,
His senses poisoned by the strange perfume,
Beholds with fierce desire the picture fair,
And grasps at nothing in the painted air,—
Gave acquiescence, in a fatal hour,
And wealth, and hope, and peace were in the
        tempter's power.
The isle became a rendezvous; and then
Came in the noisy rule of lawless men.
Domestic calm, affrighted, fled afar,
And Riot revelled 'neath the midnight star;
Continuous music rustled through the trees,
Where banners danced responsive on the breeze;
Or in festoons, above the astonished bowers,
With flaming colors shamed the modest flowers.
There clanged the mimic combat of the sword,

Like daily glasses round the festive board;
Here lounged the chiefs, there marched the plumèd
 file,
And martial splendor overran the isle.
Already, the shrewd leader of the sport
In dreams, or waking, revelling or alone,
Before him swam the visionary throne;
Until a voice, as if the insulted woods
Had risen to claim their ancient solitudes,
Broke on his spirit, like a trumpet rude,
Shattering his dream to nothing where he stood!
The revellers vanished, and the banners fell
Like the red leaves beneath November's spell.
Full of great hopes, sustained by mighty will,
Urged by ambition, confident of skill,
As fearless to perform as to devise,
A-flush, but now he saw the glittering prize
Flame like a cloud in day's descending track;
But, lo, the sun went down and left it black!
Alone, despised, defiance in his eye,
He heard the shout, and "treason!" was the cry;
And that harsh word, with its unpitying blight,
Swept o'er the island like an arctic night.
Cold grew the hearthstone, withered fell the flowers,
And moon look in as through dull prison bars.
This was the mansion. Through the ruined hall
The loud winds sweep, with gusty rise and fall,
Or glide, like phantoms, through the open doors;
And winter drifts his snow along the floors,
Blown through the yawning rafters, where the stars
and moon look in as through dull prison bars.
On yonder gable, through the nightly dark,
The owl replies unto the dreary bark
Of lonely fox, beside the grass-grown sill;
And here, on summer eves, the whip-poor-will

Exalts her voice, and to the traveller's ear
Proclaims how Ruin rules with full contentment here.

THOMAS BUCHANAN READ [1822-1872]

> Blennerhassett's Island still stands in the middle of the Ohio
> River, two miles below Parkersburg, West Virginia. Harmon
> Blennerhasset seems to have been an innocent tool in the con-
> fused conspiracy that ended Burr's turbulent career. General
> James Wilkinson, as deeply involved in the conspiracy as any-
> one, made the first allegations that led to Burr's downfall, but no
> one, to this day, knows whether Burr was out for personal em-
> pire or simply a man with a premature dream of expanding the
> brand-new United States.

★★★★★★★

England had been forced to give her American colonies
their independence, but she still harassed our ships on
the high seas. It was largely to protect our essential com-
mercial freedom that we went to war with England in
1812. Francis Scott Key, putting into verse his thoughts
on the British naval bombardment of Fort McHenry in
Baltimore, gave us a national anthem. A Tennessee mili-
tiaman, Andrew Jackson, lined up woodsmen, militia,
pirates and regular army to defeat General Sir Edward
Pakenham's British regulars at New Orleans in 1815;
ironically, the battle took place two weeks after the peace
treaty had been signed in far-away Ghent, Belgium. The
city of Washington, our unfinished new capital, was
burned, but Dolley Madison, the president's wife, res-
cued at least some valuables from the White House, and
the city set about rebuilding with energy.

The Star-Spangled Banner
☆

O say, can you see, by the dawn's early light,
What so proudly we hailed at the twilight's last gleaming?
Whose broad stripes and bright stars through the perilous
  fight,
O'er the ramparts we watched were so gallantly streaming!
And the rockets' red glare, the bombs bursting in air,
Gave proof through the night that our flag was still there.
O, say, does that star-spangled banner yet wave
O'er the land of the free, and the home of the brave?

On the shore, dimly seen through the mists of the deep,
Where the foe's haughty host in dread silence reposes,
What is that which the breeze, o'er the towering steep,
As it fitfully blows, half conceals, half discloses?
Now it catches the gleam of the morning's first beam,
In full glory reflected, now shines on the stream.
'Tis the star-spangled banner; O long may it wave
O'er the land of the free, and the home of the brave!

And where is that band who so vauntingly swore
That the havoc of war and the battle's confusion
A home and country should leave us no more?
Their blood has washed out their foul footsteps' pollution.
No refuge could save the hireling and slave
From the terror of flight, or the gloom of the grave:
And the star-spangled banner in triumph doth wave
O'er the land of the free, and the home of the brave!

Oh! thus be it ever, when freemen shall stand
Between their loved homes and the war's desolation!
Blest with victory and peace, may the heaven-rescued
  land

Praise the Power that hath made and preserved us
    a nation!
Then conquer we must, for our cause it is just,
And this be our motto: "In God is our trust."
And the star-spangled banner in triumph shall wave,
O'er the land of the free, and the home of the brave.

FRANCIS SCOTT KEY [1779-1843]

36336

The Battle of New Orleans
☆

Here, in my rude log cabin,
Few poorer men there be
Among the mountain ranges
Of Eastern Tennessee,
My limbs are weak and shrunken,
White hairs upon my brow,
My dog,—lie still old fellow!—
My sole companion now.
Yet I, when young and lusty,
Have gone through stirring scenes,
For I went down with Carroll
To fight at New Orleans.

You say you'd like to hear me
The stirring story tell,
Of those who stood the battle
And those who fighting fell.
Short work to count our losses—
We stood and dropped the foe
As easily as by firelight
Men shoot the buck or doe.
And while they fell by hundreds
Upon the bloody plain,
Of us, fourteen were wounded
And only eight were slain.

The eighth of January,
Before the break of day,
Our raw and hasty levies
Were brought into array.
No cotton-bales before us—
Some fool that falsehood told;

Before us was an earthwork
Built from the swampy mould,
And there we stood in silence,
And waited with a frown,
To greet with bloody welcome
The bull-dogs of the Crown.

The heavy fog of morning
Still hid the plain from sight,
When came a thread of scarlet
Marked faintly in the white,
We fired a single cannon,
And as its thunders rolled,
The mist before us lifted
In many a heavy fold—
The mist before us lifted
And in their bravery fine
Came rushing to their ruin
The fearless British line.

Then from our waiting cannon
Leaped forth the deadly flame,
To meet the advancing columns
That swift and steady came.
The thirty-twos of Crowley
And Bluchi's twenty-four
To Spotts's eighteen-pounders
Responded with their roar,
Sending the grape-shot deadly
That marked its pathway plain,
And paved the road it travelled
With corpses of the slain.

Our rifles firmly grasping,
And heedless of the din,
We stood in silence waiting

For orders to begin.
Our fingers on the triggers,
Our hearts, with anger stirred,
Grew still more fierce and eager
As Jackson's voice was heard:
"Stand steady! Waste no powder!
Wait till your shots will tell!
To-day the work you finish—
See that you do it well!"

Their columns drawing nearer,
We felt our patience tire,
When came the voice of Carroll,
Distinct and measured, "Fire!"
Oh! then you should have marked us
Our volleys on them pour—
Have heard our joyous rifles
Ring sharply through the roar,
And seen their foremost columns
Melt hastily away
As snow in mountain gorges
Before the floods of May.

They soon re-formed their columns,
And, mid the fatal rain
We never ceased to hurtle,
Came to their work again.
The Forty-fourth is with them,
That first its laurels won
With stout old Abercrombie
Beneath an eastern sun.
It rushes to the battle,
And, though within the rear
Its leader is a laggard,
It shows no signs of fear.

It did not need its colonel,
For soon there came instead
An eagle-eyed commander,
And on its march he led.
'Twas Pakenham in person,
The leader of the field;
I knew it by the cheering
That loudly round him pealed;
And by his quick, sharp movement
We felt his heart was stirred,
As when at Salamanca
He led the fighting Third.

. . . .

Sir Edward's charger staggers;
He leaps at once to ground.
And ere the beast falls bleeding
Another horse is found.
His right arm falls—'tis wounded;
He waves on high his left;
In vain he leads the movement,
The ranks in twain are cleft.
The men in scarlet waver
Before the men in brown,
And fly in utter panic—
The soldiers of the Crown!

. . . .

The smoke passed slowly upward
And, as it soared on high,
I saw the brave commander
In dying anguish lie.
They bear him from the battle
Who never fled the foe;
Unmoved by death around them

His bearers softly go.
In vain their care, so gentle,
Fades earth and all its scenes;
The man of Salamanca
Lies dead at New Orleans.

. . . .

The stormers had retreated,
The bloody work was o'er;
The feet of the invaders
Were soon to leave our shore.
We rested on our rifles
And talked about the fight,
When came a sudden murmur
Like fire from left to right;
We turned and saw our chieftain,
And then, good friend of mine,
You should have heard the cheering
That rang along the line.

For well our men remembered
How little, when they came,
Had they but native courage,
And trust in Jackson's name;
How through the day he labored,
How kept the vigils still,
Till discipline controlled us—
A stronger power than will;
And how he hurled us at them
Within the evening hour,
That red night in December
And made us feel our power.

In answer to our shouting
Fire lit his eye of gray;

Erect, but thin and pallid,
He passed upon his bay.
Weak from the baffled fever,
And shrunken in each limb,
The swamps of Alabama
Had done their work on him;
But spite of that and fasting,
And hours of sleepless care,
The soul of Andrew Jackson
Shone forth in glory there.

THOMAS DUNN ENGLISH [1819-1902]

The Battle of New Orleans was fought two weeks after the
Treaty of Ghent had actually ended the War of 1812. Slow
communications kept the news of peace from the warring armies
until the battle, which settled nothing except the emergence of
Andrew Jackson as a new American hero, was over.

★★★★★★★

The whole country was growing. New England skippers
like poor Ireson (whom Whittier later learned had *not*
deserted his drowning seamen) were carrying cargo to
and from all the commercial ports of the world. Thomas
Jefferson died in 1826 and Lafayette, the French noble
who had thrown in his lot with the American Revolu-
tion, was memorialized on his death in 1834 in verses
by Mrs. Madison. Oliver Wendell Holmes (writing con-
siderably later to protest its planned destruction) im-
mortalized *Old Ironsides,* the heroic surviving frigate of
the War of 1812.

The young country was much too busy to appreciate the work of one of its artists; John James Audubon had to go to the scientific and cultural leaders of London and Edinburgh to get financial backing for his great work, *The Birds of America.*

Skipper Ireson's Ride
☆

Of all the rides since the birth of time,
Told in story or sung in rhyme,—
On Apuleius's Golden Ass,
Or one-eyed Calendar's horse of brass,
Witch astride of a human back,
Islam's prophet on Al-Borák,—
The strangest ride that ever was sped
Was Ireson's, out from Marblehead!
Old Floyd Ireson, for his hard heart,
Tarred and feathered and carried in a cart
By the women of Marblehead!

Body of turkey, head of owl,
Wings a-droop like a rained-on fowl,
Feathered and ruffled in every part,
Skipper Ireson stood in the cart.
Scores of women, old and young,
Strong of muscle, and glib of tongue,
Pushed and pulled up the rocky lane,
Shouting and singing the shrill refrain:
"Here's Flud Oirson, fur his horrd horrt,
Torr'd an' futherr'd an' corr'd in a corrt
By the women o' Morble'ead!"

Wrinkled scolds with hands on hips,
Girls in bloom of cheek and lips,
Wild-eyed, free-limbed, such as chase
Bacchus round some antique vase,
Brief of skirt, with ankles bare,
Loose of kerchief and loose of hair,
With conch-shells blowing and fish-horns' twang,
Over and over the Maenads sang:
"Here's Flud Oirson, fur his horrd horrt,
Torr'd an' futherr'd an' corr'd in a corrt
By the women o' Morble'ead!"

Small pity for him!—He sailed away
From a leaking ship in Chaleur Bay,—
Sailed away from a sinking wreck,
With his own town's-people on her deck!
"Lay by! lay by!" they called to him.
Back he answered, "Sink or swim!
Brag of your catch of fish again!"
And off he sailed through the fog and rain!
Old Floyd Ireson, for his hard heart,
Tarred and feathered and carried in a cart
By the women of Marblehead!

Fathoms deep in dark Chaleur
That wreck shall lie forevermore.
Mother and sister, wife and maid,
Looked from the rocks of Marblehead
Over the moaning and rainy sea,—
Looked for the coming that might not be!
What did the winds and the sea-birds say
Of the cruel captain who sailed away?—
Old Floyd Ireson, for his hard heart,
Tarred and feathered and carried in a cart
By the women of Marblehead!

Through the street, on either side,
Up flew windows, doors swung wide;
Sharp-tongued spinsters, old wives gray,
Treble lent the fish-horn's bray.
Sea-worn grandsires, cripple-bound,
Hulks of old sailors run aground,
Shook head, and fist, and hat, and cane,
And cracked with curses the hoarse refrain:
"Here's Flud Oirson, fur his horrd horrt,
Torr'd an' futherr'd an' corr'd in a corrt
By the women o' Morble'ead!"

· · · · · · · · · · · ·

"Hear me, neighbors!" at last he cried,—
"What to me is this noisy ride?
What is the shame that clothes the skin
To the nameless horror that lives within?
Waking or sleeping, I see a wreck,
And hear a cry from a reeling deck!
Hate me and curse me,—I only dread
The hand of God and the face of the dead!"
Said old Floyd Ireson, for his hard heart,
Tarred and feathered and carried in a cart
By the women of Marblehead!

Then the wife of the skipper lost at sea
Said, "God has touched him! why should we!"
Said an old wife mourning her only son,
"Cut the rogue's tether and let him run!"
So with soft relentings and rude excuse,
Half scorn, half pity, they cut him loose,
And gave him a cloak to hide him in,
And left him alone with his shame and sin.
Poor Floyd Ireson, for his hard heart,
Tarred and feathered and carried in a cart
By the women of Marblehead!

JOHN GREENLEAF WHITTIER [1807-1892]

The Death of Jefferson
☆

I

'Twas midsummer; cooling breezes all the languid forests
    fanned,
And the angel of the evening drew her curtain o'er the
    land.

Like an isle rose Monticello through the cooled and
    rippling trees,
Like an isle in rippling starlight in the silence of the seas.
Ceased the mocking-bird his singing; said the slaves with
    faltering breath,
" 'Tis the Third, and on the morrow Heaven will send the
    Angel Death."

II

In his room at Monticello, lost in dreams the statesman
    slept,
Seeing not the still forms round him, seeing not the eyes
    that wept,
Hearing not the old clock ticking in life's final silence loud,
Knowing not when night came o'er him like the shadow of
    a cloud.
In the past his soul is living as in fifty years ago,
Hastes again to Philadelphia, hears again the Schuylkill
    flow—

III

Meets again the elder Adams—knowing not that far away
He is waiting for Death's morrow, on old Massachusetts
    Bay;
Meets with Hancock, young and courtly, meets with
    Hopkins, bent and old,
Meets again calm Roger Sherman, fiery Lee, and Carroll
    bold,
Meets the sturdy form of Franklin, meets the half a
    hundred men
Who have made themselves immortal,—breathes the
    ancient morn again.

IV

Once again the Declaration in his nerveless hands he
  holds,
And before the waiting statesmen its prophetic hope
  unfolds,—
Reads again the words puissant, "All men are created
  free,"
Claims again for man his birthright, claims the world's
  equality;
Hears the coming and the going of an hundred firm-set
  feet,
Hears the summer breezes blowing 'mid the oak trees cool
  and sweet.

V

Sees again tall Patrick Henry by the side of Henry Lee,
Hears him cry, "And will ye sign it?—it will make all
  nations free!
Fear ye not the axe or gibbet; it shall topple every throne.
Sign it for the world's redemption!—all mankind its truth
  shall own!
Stars may fall, but truth eternal shall not falter, shall not
  fail.
Sign it, and the Declaration shall the voice of ages hail."

VI

"Sign, and set yon dumb bell ringing, that the people all
  may know
Man has found emancipation; sign, the Almighty wills it
  so."
Sees one sign it, then another, till like magic moves the
  pen,
Till all have signed it, and it lies there, Charter of the
  rights of men.

Hears the small bells, hears the great bell, hanging idly in
    the sun,
Break the silence, and the people whisper, awe-struck, "It
    is done."

VII

Then the dream began to vanish—burgesses, the war's red
    flames,
Charging Tarleton, proud Cornwallis, navies moving on the
    James,
Years of peace, and years of glory, all began to melt away,
And the statesman woke from slumber in the night, and
    tranquil lay,
And his lips moved; friends there gathered with love's
    silken footstep near,
And he whispered, softly whispered in love's low and
    tender ear,—

VIII

"It is the Fourth?" "No, not yet," they answered, "but 't
    will soon be early morn;
We will wake you, if you slumber, when the day begins to
    dawn."
Then the statesman left the present, lived again amid the
    past,
Saw, perhaps, the peopled future ope its portals grand and
    vast,
Till the flashes of the morning lit the far horizon low,
And the sun's rays o'er the forests in the east began to
    glow.

IX

Rose the sun, and from the woodlands, fell the midnight
    dews like rain,

In magnolias cool and shady sang the mocking-bird again;
And the statesman woke from slumber, saw the risen sun,
    and heard
Rippling breezes 'mid the oak trees, and the lattice singing
    bird,
And, his eye serene uplifted, as rejoicing in the sun,
"It is the Fourth?" his only question,—to the world his
    final one.

    x

Silence fell on Monticello—for the last dread hour was
    near,
And the old clock's measured ticking only broke upon the
    ear.
All the summer rooms were silent, where the great of earth
    had trod,
All the summer blooms seemed silent as the messengers of
    God;
Silent were the hall and chamber where old councils oft
    had met,
Save the far boom of the cannon that recalled the old day
    yet.

    XI

Silent still is Monticello—he is breathing slowly now,
In the splendors of the noon-tide, with the death-dew on
    his brow—
Silent save the clock still ticking where his soul had given
    birth
To the mighty thoughts of freedom, that should free the
    fettered earth;
Silent save the boom of cannon on the sun-filled wave afar,
Bringing 'mid the peace eternal still the memory of war.

XII

Evening in majestic shadows fell upon the fortress' walls;
Sweetly were the last bells ringing on the James and on
the Charles.
'Mid the choruses of freedom two departed victors lay,
One beside the blue Rivanna, one by Massachusetts Bay.
He was gone, and night her sable curtain drew across the
sky;
Gone his soul into all nations, gone to live and not to die.

HEZEKIAH BUTTERWORTH [1837-1905]

La Fayette
☆

Born, nurtured, wedded, prized, within the pale
Of peers and princes, high in camp—at court—
He hears, in joyous youth, a wild report,
Swelling the murmurs of the Western gale,
Of a young people struggling to be free!
Straight quitting all, across the wave he flies,
Aids with his sword, wealth, blood, the high emprize!
And shares the glories of its victory.
Then comes for fifty years a high romance
Of toils, reverses, sufferings, in the cause
Of man and justice, liberty and France,
Crowned, at the last, with hope and wide applause.
Champion of Freedom! Well thy race was run!
All time shall hail thee, Europe's noblest Son!

DOLLEY MADISON [1768-1849]

Old Ironsides

☆

Ay, tear her tattered ensign down!
Long has it waved on high,
And many an eye has danced to see
That banner in the sky;
Beneath it rung the battle shout,
And burst the cannon's roar;—
The meteor of the ocean air
Shall sweep the clouds no more!

Her deck, once red with heroes' blood,
Where knelt the vanquished foe,
When winds were hurrying o'er the flood,
And waves were white below,
No more shall feel the victor's tread,
Or know the conquered knee;—
The harpies of the shore shall pluck
The eagle of the sea!

Oh better that her shattered hulk
Should sink beneath the wave;
Her thunders shook the mighty deep,
And there should be her grave;
Nail to the mast her holy flag,
Set every threadbare sail,
And give her to the god of storms,
The lightning and the gale!

OLIVER WENDELL HOLMES [1809-1894]

John James Audubon
1780-1851

☆

Some men live for warlike deeds,
Some for women's words.

John James Audubon
Lived to look at birds.

Pretty birds and funny birds,
All our native fowl
From the little cedar waxwing
To the Great Horned Owl.

Let the wind blow hot or cold,
Let it rain or snow,
Everywhere the birds went
Audubon would go.

Scrambling through a wilderness,
Floating down a stream,
All around America
In a feathered dream.

Thirty years of traveling,
Pockets often bare,
(Lucy Bakewell Audubon
Patched them up with care.)

Followed grebe and meadowlark,
Saw them sing and splash.
(Lucy Bakewell Audubon
Somehow raised the cash.)

Drew them all the way they lived
In their habitats.
(Lucy Bakewell Audubon
Sometimes wondered "Cats?")

Colored them and printed them
In a giant book,
"Birds of North America"—
All the world said, "Look!"

Gave him medals and degrees,
Called him noble names,
—Lucy Bakewell Audubon
Kissed her queer John James.

STEPHEN VINCENT BENÉT [1898-1943]

★★★★★★★

There were still settlers turning the wilderness into farms and townsites from Ohio west. There were still wars; disturbances in the southwest where the Republic of Texas cut itself away from Mexico, continuing Indian wars where William Henry Harrison won his nickname of "Old Tippecanoe" by defeating the Shawnee Chief Tecumseh. This victory was to help General Harrison in his successful campaign for the presidency in 1840.

Harrison died before real war broke out with Mexico, although border troubles had been increasing even before 1845, the date when the Texans had voted to join the Union. War was declared against Mexico in 1846. It was a short and successful campaign with only moderate losses and a list of new battle-names like Monterey to stand in the lists of national victories.

It was in some unexpected ways a war of rehearsal for a longer, bloodier, more squalid and more glorious war to come. The Mexican War gave young officers named Grant and Lee, Sherman and Longstreet their first taste of action.

The Founders of Ohio
☆

The footsteps of a hundred years
Have echoed, since o'er Braddock's Road
Bold Putnam and the Pioneers
Led History the way they strode.

On wild Monongahela stream
They launched the Mayflower of the West,
A perfect State their civic dream,
A new New World their pilgrim quest.

When April robed the Buckeye trees
Muskingum's bosky shore they trod;
They pitched their tents, and to the breeze
Flung freedom's star-flag, thanking God.

As glides the Oyo's solemn flood,
So fleeted their eventful years;
Resurgent in their children's blood,
They still live on—the Pioneers.

Their fame shrinks not to names and dates
On votive stone, the prey of time;—
Behold where monumental States
Immortalize their lives sublime!

WILLIAM HENRY VENABLE [1836-1920]

The Men of the Alamo
☆

To Houston at Gonzales town, ride, Ranger, for your life,
Nor stop to say good-bye to-day to home, or child, or wife;
But pass the word from ranch to ranch, to every Texan
    sword,
That fifty hundred Mexicans have crossed the Nueces ford,
With Castrillon and perjured Cos, Sesmá and Almontê,
And Santa Anna ravenous for vengeance and for prey!
They smite the land with fire and sword; the grass shall
    never grow
Where northward sweeps that locust herd on San Antonio!

Now who will bar the foeman's path, to gain a breathing
    space,
Till Houston and his scattered men shall meet him face to
    face?
Who holds his life as less than naught when home and
    honor call,
And counts the guerdon full and fair for liberty to fall?
Oh, who but Barrett Travis, the bravest of them all!
With seven score of riflemen to play the rancher's game,
And feed a counter-fire to halt the sweeping prairie flame;
For Bowie of the broken blade is there to cheer them on,
With Evans of Concepcion, who conquered Castrillon,
And o'er their heads the Lone Star flag defiant floats on
    high,
And no man thinks of yielding, and no man fears to die.

But ere the siege is held a week a cry is heard without,
A clash of arms, a rifle peal, the Ranger's ringing shout,
And two-and-thirty beardless boys have bravely hewed
    their way
To die with Travis if they must, to conquer if they may.

Was ever valor held so cheap in Glory's mart before
In all the days of chivalry, in all the deeds of war?

But once again the foemen gaze in wonderment and fear
To see a stranger break their lines and hear the Texans
    cheer.
God! how they cheered to welcome him, those spent and
    starving men!
For Davy Crockett by their side was worth an army then.
The wounded ones forgot their wounds; the dying drew a
    breath
To hail the king of border men, then turned to laugh at
    death.
For all knew Davy Crockett, blithe and generous as bold,
And strong and rugged as the quartz that hides its heart of
    gold.
His simple creed for word or deed true as the bullet sped,
And rung the target straight: "Be sure you're right, then
    go ahead!"

And were they right who fought the fight for Texas by his
    side?
They questioned not; they faltered not; they only fought
    and died.
Who hath an enemy like these, God's mercy slay him
    straight!—
A thousand Mexicans lay dead outside the convent gate.
And half a thousand more must die before the fortress
    falls,
And still the tide of war beats high around the leaguered
    walls.
At last the bloody breach is won; the weakened lines give
    way;
The wolves are swarming in the court; the lions stand at
    bay.

The leader meets them at the breach, and wins the
    soldier's prize;
A foeman's bosom sheathes his sword when gallant Travis
    dies.

Now let the victor feast at will until his crest be red—

We may not know what raptures fill the vulture with the
    dead.
Let Santa Anna's valiant sword right bravely hew and
    hack
The senseless corpse; its hands are cold; they will not
    strike him back.
Let Bowie die, but 'ware the hand that wields his deadly
    knife;
Four went to slay, and one comes back so dear he sells his
    life.
And last of all let Crockett fall, too proud to sue for grace,
So grand in death the butcher dared not look upon his
    face.

But far on San Jacinto's field the Texan toils are set,
And Alamo's dread memory the Texan steel shall whet.
And Fame shall tell their deeds who fell till all the years
    be run.
"Thermopylae left one alive—the Alamo left none."

JAMES JEFFREY ROCHE [1847-1908]

Old Tippecanoe
☆

Come, rouse up, ye bold-hearted Whigs of Kentucky,
And show the nation what deeds you can do;
The high-road to victory lies open before ye
While led to the charge by Old Tippecanoe.

When Indians were scalping our friends and our brothers,
To Ohio's frontier he gallantly flew;
And thousands of innocent infants, and mothers,
Were saved by the valor of Tippecanoe.

When savage Tecumseh was rallying his forces,
In innocent blood his hands to imbrue;
Our hero despis'd all his bloody associates,
And won the proud name of Old Tippecanoe.

And when this Tecumseh and his brother Proctor,
To capture Fort Meigs their utmost did do;
Our gallant old hero again play'd the Doctor,
And gave them a dose like at Tippecanoe.

And then on the Thames, on the fifth of October,
Where musket balls whizz'd as they flew;
He blasted their prospects, and rent them asunder,
Just like he had done on the Tippecanoe.

Let Greece praise the deeds of her great Alexander
And Rome boast of Caesar and Scipio too;
Just like Cincinnatus, that noble commander,
Is our old Hero of Tippecanoe.

For when the foes of his country no longer could harm
  her,
To the shades of retirement he quickly withdrew;
And now at North Bend see the Honest Old Farmer,
Who won the green laurel at Tippecanoe.

And when to the National Council elected,
The good of his country still see him pursue,
And every poor man by him thus protected,
Should ever remember "Old Tippecanoe."

And now from retirement the People doth call him,
Because he is Honest and Qualified too;
And for One Full Term they soon will install him
As President—"Hero of Tippecanoe."

. . . .

Among the supporters of brave General Jackson,
There are many Republicans, honest and true,
To all such we say "come out from among them,"
And "go it for" Tyler and "Tippecanoe."

ANONYMOUS

Tyler was the vice president. Harrison and Tyler's campaign
slogan was "Tippecanoe and Tyler too."

Monterey
☆

We were not many, we who stood
Before the iron sleet that day:
Yet many a gallant spirit would
Give half his years if but he would
Have been with us at Monterey.

Now here, now there, the shot is hail'd
In deadly drifts of fiery spray,
Yet not a single soldier quail'd
When wounded comrades round them wail'd
Their dying shout at Monterey.

And on—still on our column kept
Through walls of flame its withering way;
Where fell the dead, the living stept,
Still charging on the guns which swept
The slippery streets of Monterey.

The foe himself recoil'd aghast,
When, striking where he strongest lay,
We swooped his flanking batteries past,
And braving full their murderous blast,
Storm'd home the towers of Monterey.

Our banners on those turrets wave,
And there our evening bugles play:
Where orange-boughs above their grave
Keep green the memory of the brave
Who fought and fell at Monterey.

We are not many—we who press'd
Beside the brave who fell that day—
But who of us has not confess'd
He'd rather share their warrior rest
Than not have been at Monterey?

CHARLES FENNO HOFFMAN [1806-1884]

A NATION DIVIDED

THE GREATEST GROWING PAIN of the new nation was the ugly problem of slavery. Slavery as an institution had been abolished throughout almost all of the civilized world, but the southern half of the United States clung to it because of the cheap labor thought necessary to its vital investment in cotton. The South had made threats of secession and Daniel Webster, the golden-tongued congressional lawyer, had effectively used his power of persuasion to hold the Union together by emotion and careful compromise. This was a land of freedom *and* union and should so hold together. The new nation should not be allowed to split because of a difference of opinion, even when the difference concerned a basic issue of human freedom.

But split it did, and the split was almost permanent. As Abraham Lincoln campaigned for the White House on a hopeful platform of moderation, John Brown, a radical abolitionist, raided the government arsenal at Harpers Ferry, Virginia, to help arm slaves against their masters. Federal troops led by Colonel Robert E. Lee captured Brown and he was turned over to the state of Virginia for trial and execution. But the spark he had kindled would not die.

And, on the opposite side, seven southern states had

already left the Union by the time of Lincoln's inauguration in 1861. Divisionist spirits on both sides fed on heady songs of righteous wrath. Poets could lament the loss of sister states, but when a sister state fired on the American flag at Fort Sumter, things had gone too far for peaceful patching up.

Nancy Hanks, Mother of Abraham Lincoln
☆

"Out of the eater came forth meat; and out of the strong came forth sweetness."   JUDGES 14:14

A sweet girl graduate, lean as a fawn,
The very whimsy of time,
Read her class poem Commencement Day—
A trembling filigree rhyme.

The pansy that blooms on the window sill,
Blooms in exactly the proper place;
And she nodded just like a pansy there,
And her poem was all about bowers and showers,
Sugary streamlet and mossy rill,
All about daisies on dale and hill—
And she was the mother of Buffalo Bill.

Another girl, a cloud-drift sort,
Dreamlit, moonlit, marble-white,

Light-footed saint on the pilgrim shore,
The best since New England fairies began,
Was the mother of Barnum, the circus man.

A girl from Missouri, snippy and vain,
As frothy a miss as any you know,
A wren, a toy, a pink silk bow,
The belle of the choir, she drove insane
Missouri deacons and all the sleek,
Her utter tomfoolery made men weak,
Till they could not stand and they could not speak.
Oh, queen of fifteen and sixteen,
Missouri sweetened beneath her reign—
And she was the mother of bad Mark Twain.

Not always are lions born of lions,
Roosevelt sprang from a palace of lace;
On the other hand is the dizzy truth:
Not always is beauty born of beauty.
Some treasures wait in a hidden place.
All over the world were thousands of belles.
In far-off eighteen hundred and nine,
Girls of fifteen, girls of twenty,
Their mammas dressed them up a-plenty—
Each garter was bright, each stocking fine,
But for all their innocent devices,
Their cheeks of fruit and their eyes of wine,
And each voluptuous design,
And all soft glories that we trace
In Europe's palaces of lace,
A girl who slept in dust and sorrow,
Nancy Hanks, in a lost log cabin,
Nancy Hanks had the loveliest face!

VACHEL LINDSAY [1879-1931]

Brown of Ossawatomie
☆

John Brown of Ossawatomie spake on his dying day:
"I will not have to shrive my soul a priest in Slavery's pay.
But let some poor slave-mother whom I have striven to
    free,
With her children, from the gallows-stair put up a prayer
    for me!"

John Brown of Ossawatomie, they led him out to die;
And lo! a poor slave-mother with her little child pressed
    nigh.
Then the bold, blue eye grew tender, and the old harsh
    face grew mild,
As he stooped between the jeering ranks and kissed the
    Negro's child!

The shadows of his stormy life that moment fell apart;
And they who blamed the bloody hand forgave the loving
    heart.
That kiss from all its guilty means redeemed the good
    intent,
And round the grisly fighter's hair the martyr's aureole
    bent!

Perish with him the folly that seeks through evil good!
Long live the generous purpose unstained with human
    blood!
Not the raid of midnight terror, but the thought which
    underlies;
Not the borderer's pride of daring, but the Christian's
    sacrifice.

Nevermore may yon Blue Ridges the Northern rifle hear,

Nor see the light of blazing homes flash on the Negro's
    spear,
But let the free-winged angel Truth their guarded passes
    scale,
To teach that right is more than might, and justice more
    than mail!

So vainly shall Virginia set her battle in array;
In vain her trampling squadrons knead the winter snow
    with clay.
She may strike the pouncing eagle, but she dares not harm
    the dove;
And every gate she bars to Hate shall open wide to Love!

JOHN GREENLEAF WHITTIER [1809-1892]

Glory Hallelujah! *or* John Brown's Body
☆

John Brown's body lies a-mouldering in the grave,
John Brown's body lies a-mouldering in the grave,
John Brown's body lies a-mouldering in the grave,
    But his soul goes marching on!

    Glory! Glory Hallelujah!
    Glory! Glory Hallelujah!
    Glory! Glory Hallelujah!
        His soul goes marching on!

He has gone to be a soldier in the army of the Lord!
He has gone to be a soldier in the army of the Lord!
He has gone to be a soldier in the army of the Lord!
    But his soul goes marching on!

Glory! Glory Hallelujah!
Glory! Glory Hallelujah!
Glory! Glory Hallelujah!
    His soul goes marching on!

ANONYMOUS

Battle-Hymn of the Republic
☆

Mine eyes have seen the glory of the coming of the Lord:
He is trampling out the vintage where the grapes of wrath
    are stored;
He hath loosed the fateful lightning of his terrible swift
    sword:
His truth is marching on.

I have seen Him in the watch-fires of a hundred circling
    camps;
They have builded Him an altar in the evening dews and
    damps;
I can read his righteous sentence by the dim and flaring
    lamps
His day is marching on.

I have read a fiery gospel, writ in burnished rows of steel:
"As ye deal with my contemners, so with you my grace
    shall deal;
Let the Hero, born of woman, crush the serpent with his
    heel,
Since God is marching on."

He has sounded forth the trumpet that shall never call
    retreat;

He is sifting out the hearts of men before his judgment-
    seat;
Oh! be swift, my soul, to answer Him! be jubilant, my
    feet!
Our God is marching on.

In the beauty of the lilies Christ was born across the sea,
With a glory in his bosom that transfigures you and me:
As He died to make men holy, let us die to make men
    free,
While God is marching on.

JULIA WARD HOWE [1819-1910]

The Bonnie Blue Flag
☆

Come, brothers! rally for the right!
The bravest of the brave
Sends forth her ringing battle-cry
Beside the Atlantic wave!
She leads the way in honor's path;
Come, brothers, near and far,
Come rally round the Bonnie Blue Flag
That bears a single star!

We've borne the Yankee trickery,
The Yankee gibe and sneer,
Till Yankee insolence and pride
Know neither shame nor fear;
But ready now with shot and steel
Their brazen front to mar
We hoist aloft the Bonnie Blue Flag
That bears a single star.

Now Georgia marches to the front,
And close beside her come
Her sisters by the Mexique Sea,
With pealing trump and drum;
Till answering back from hill and glen
The rallying cry afar,
A Nation hoists the Bonnie Blue Flag
That bears a single star.

By every stone in Charleston Bay,
By each beleaguered town,
We swear to rest not, night nor day,
But hunt the tyrants down!
Till bathed in valor's holy blood
The gazing world afar
Shall greet with shouts the Bonnie Blue Flag
That bears the cross and star!

ANNIE CHAMBERS KETCHUM [1824-1904]

Brother Jonathan's Lament for Sister Caroline
☆

She has gone,—she has left us in passion and pride,—
Our stormy-browed sister, so long at our side!
She has torn her own star from our firmament's glow,
And turned on her brother the face of a foe!

O Caroline, Caroline, child of the sun,
We can never forget that our hearts have been one,—
Our foreheads both sprinkled in Liberty's name,
From the fountain of blood with the finger of flame!

You were always too ready to fire at a touch;
But we said: "She is hasty,—she does not mean much."
We have scowled when you uttered some turbulent
    threat;
But Friendship still whispered: "Forgive and forget."

Has our love all died out? Have its altars grown cold?
Has the curse come at last which the fathers foretold?
Then Nature must teach us the strength of the chain
That her petulant children would sever in vain.

They may fight till the buzzards are gorged with their
    spoil,—
Till the harvest grows black as it rots in the soil,
Till the wolves and the catamounts troop from their
    caves,
And the shark tracks the pirate, the lord of the waves:

In vain is the strife! When its fury is past,
Their fortunes must flow in one channel at last,
As the torrents that rush from the mountains of snow
Roll mingled in peace through the valleys below.

Our Union is river, lake, ocean, and sky;
Man breaks not the medal when God cuts the die!
Though darkened with sulphur, though cloven with steel,
The blue arch will brighten, the waters will heal!

O Caroline, Caroline, child of the sun,
There are battles with fate that can never be won!
The star-flowering banner must never be furled,
For its blossoms of light are the hope of the world!

Go, then, our rash sister, afar and aloof,—
Run wild in the sunshine away from our roof;
But when your heart aches and your feet have grown sore,
Remember the pathway that leads to our door!

OLIVER WENDELL HOLMES [1809-1894]

Brother Jonathan was a popular nickname for the United States, predating Uncle Sam, and Sister Caroline stood for the seceding Carolinas.

★★★★★★★

The Civil War was the longest, saddest trial that the United States had yet had to meet. For four years former friends and even relatives slaughtered one another across a nation that now stretched from the Atlantic to the Pacific (California had become a state in 1850). Admiral Farrugut took New Orleans for the Union in 1862, and the Union *Monitor* defeated the Confederate *Merrimack* in the same year, but these were only events on the periphery of the long land struggle. There was gallantry, as in Stonewall Jackson's courtesy to Barbara Frietchie (the lady in question was actually named Mrs. Mary A. Quantrell), and pathos in Jackson's own death in battle. There were moments of high heroism and suspense. There were also misery, cruelty and bungling on both sides. Over all was the gaunt, sad, wise figure of Abraham Lincoln, whose death still stands as a national tragedy unmatched by any other moment in our history.

From John Brown's Body
☆

It was noon when the company marched to the railroad-
    station.
The town was ready for them. The streets were packed.
There were flags and streamers and pictures of Lincoln
    and Hamlin.
The bad little boys climbed up on the trees and yelled,
The good little boys had clean paper-collars on,
And swung big-eyed on white-painted wicket-gates,
Wanting to yell, and feeling like Fourth of July.
Somebody fastened a tin can full of firecrackers
To a yellow dog's tail and sent him howling and racketing
The length of the street. "There goes Jeff Davis!" said
    somebody,
And everybody laughed, and the little boys
Punched each other and squealed between fits of laughing
"There goes Jeff Davis—looket ole yellow Jeff Davis!"
And then the laugh died and rose again in a strange
Half-shrill, half-strangled unexpected shout
As they heard the Hillsboro Silver Cornet Band
Singing "John Brown's Body" ahead of the soldiers.
I have heard that soul of crowd go out in the queer
Groan between laughter and tears that baffles the wise.
I have heard that whanging band.

"We'll hang Jeff Davis on a sour-apple tree."
Double-roll on the snare-drums, double squeal of the fife,
"We'll hang Jeff Davis on a sour-apple tree!"
Clash of the cymbals zinging, throaty blare of cornets,
"We'll hang Jeff Davis on a sour-apple tree!"
"On to Richmond! On to Richmond! On to Richmond!"
"Yeah! There they come! Yeah! Yeah!"
And they came, the bearskin drum-major leading the band,

Twirling his silver-balled baton with turkey-cock pomp,
The cornet-blowers, the ranks. The drum-major was fine,
But the little boys thought the captain was even finer,
He looked just like a captain out of a book
With his sword and his shoulder-straps and his discipline-
    face.
He wasn't just Henry Fairfield, he was a captain,
—Henry Fairfield worried about his sword,
Hoping to God that he wouldn't drop his sword,
And wondering hotly whether his discipline-face
Really looked disciplined or only peevish—
"Yeah! There they come! There's Jack! There's Charlie!
    Yeah!
Yeah!"

The color-guard with the stiff, new flapping flag,
And the ranks and the ranks and the ranks, the amateur
Blue, wavering ranks, in their ill-fitting tight coats,
Shoulders galled already by their new guns,
—They were three-months' men, they had drilled in
    civilian clothes
Till a week ago—"There's Charlie! There's Hank, yeah,
    yeah!"
"On to Richmond, boys! Three cheers for Abe Lincoln!
Three cheers for the boys! Three groans for old Jeff Davis
And the dirty Rebs!"
"We'll hang Jeff Davis on a sour-apple tree!"

STEPHEN VINCENT BENÉT [1898-1943]

Farragut
☆

Farragut, Farragut,
Old Heart of Oak,
Daring Dave Farragut,
Thunderbolt stroke,
Watches the hoary mist
Lift from the bay,
Till his flag, glory-kissed,
Greets the young day.

Far, by gray Morgan's walls,
Looms the black fleet.
Hark, deck to rampart calls
With the drums' beat!
Buoy your chains overboard,
While the steam hums;
Men! to the battlement,
Farragut comes.

See, as the hurricane
Hurtles in wrath
Squadrons of clouds amain
Back from its path!
Back to the parapet,
To the guns' lips,
Thunderbolt Farragut
Hurls the black ships.

Now through the battle's roar
Clear the boy sings,
"By the mark fathoms four."

While his lead swings.
Steady the wheelmen five
"Nor' by East keep her,"
"Steady," but two alive:
How the shells sweep her!

Lashed to the mast that sways
Over the red decks
Over the flame that plays
Round the torn wrecks,
Over the dying lips
Framed for a cheer,
Farragut leads his ships,
Guides the line clear.

On by heights cannon-browed,
While the spars quiver;
Onward still flames the cloud
Where the hulks shiver.
See, yon fort's star is set,
Storm and fire past.
Cheer him, lads—Farragut,
Lashed to the mast!

Oh! while Atlantic's breast
Bears a white sail,
While the Gulf's towering crest
Tops a green vale,
Men thy bold deeds shall tell,
Old Heart of Oak,
Daring Dave Farragut,
Thunderbolt stroke!

WILLIAM TUCKER MEREDITH

The Cruise of the Monitor
☆

Out of a Northern city's bay,
'Neath lowering clouds, one bleak March day,
Glided a craft—the like, I ween,
On ocean's crest was never seen
Since Noah's float, that ancient boat,
Could o'er a conquered deluge gloat.

No raking masts, with clouds of sail,
Bent to the breeze, or braved the gale;
No towering chimney's wreaths of smoke
Betrayed the mighty engine's stroke;
But low and dark, like the crafty shark,
Moved in the waters this novel bark.

The fishers stared as the flitting sprite
Passed their huts in the misty light,
Bearing a turret huge and black,
And said, "The old sea-serpent's back,
Carting away by light of day,
Uncle Sam's fort from New York Bay."

Forth from a Southern city's dock,
Our frigates' strong blockade to mock,
Crept a monster of rugged build,
The work of crafty hands, well skilled—
Old Merrimac, with an iron back
Wooden ships would find hard to crack.

Straight to where the Cumberland lay,
The mail-clad monster made its way;
Its deadly prow struck deep and sure,
And the hero's fighting days were o'er.

Ah! many the braves who found their graves,
With that good ship, beneath the waves!

But with their fate is glory wrought,
Those hearts of oak like heroes fought
With desperate hope to win the day,
And crush the foe that 'fore them lay.
Our flag up run, the last-fired gun,
Tokens how bravely duty was done.

Flushed with success, the victor flew,
Furious, the startled squadron through:
Sinking, burning, driving ashore,
Until that Sabbath day was o'er,
Resting at night to renew the fight
With vengeful ire by morning's light.

Out of its den it burst anew,
When the gray mist the sun broke through,
Steaming to where, in clinging sands,
The frigate Minnesota stands,
A sturdy foe to overthrow,
But in woful plight to receive a blow.

But see! Beneath her bow appears
A champion no danger fears;
A pigmy craft, that seems to be
To this new lord, who rules the sea,
Like David of old to Goliath bold—
Youth and giant, by Scripture told.

Round the roaring despot playing,
With willing spirit, helm obeying,
Spurning the iron against it hurled,
While belching turret rapid whirled,

And swift shot's seethe, with smoky wreath,
Told that the shark was showing his teeth—

The Monitor fought. In grim amaze
The Merrimacs upon it gaze,
Cowering 'neath the iron hail,
Crashing into their coat of mail;
They swore "this craft, the devil's shaft,
Looked like a cheese-box on a raft."

Hurrah! little giant of '62!
Bold Worden with his gallant crew
Forces the fight; the day is won;
Back to his den the monster's gone
With crippled claws and broken jaws,
Defeated in a reckless cause.

Hurrah for the master mind that wrought,
With iron hand, this iron thought!
Strength and safety with speed combined,
Ericsson's gift to all mankind;
To curb abuse, and chains to loose,
Hurrah for the Monitor's famous cruise!

GEORGE HENRY BOKER [1823-1890]

Barbara Frietchie
☆

Up from the meadows rich with corn,
Clear in the cool September morn,

The clustered spires of Frederick stand
Green-walled by the hills of Maryland.

Round about them orchards sweep,
Apple and peach tree fruited deep,

Fair as the garden of the Lord
To the eyes of the famished rebel horde,

On that pleasant morn of the early fall
When Lee marched over the mountain-wall;

Over the mountains winding down,
Horse and foot, into Frederick town.

Forty flags with their silver stars,
Forty flags with their crimson bars,

Flapped in the morning wind: the sun
Of noon looked down, and saw not one.

Up rose old Barbara Frietchie then,
Bowed with her fourscore years and ten;

Bravest of all in Frederick town,
She took up the flag the men hauled down;

In her attic window the staff she set,
To show that one heart was loyal yet.

Up the street came the rebel tread,
Stonewall Jackson riding ahead.

Under his slouched hat left and right
He glanced; the old flag met his sight.

"Halt!"—the dust-brown ranks stood fast.
"Fire!"—out blazed the rifle-blast.

It shivered the window, pane and sash;
It rent the banner with seam and gash.

Quick, as it fell, from the broken staff
Dame Barbara snatched the silken scarf.

She leaned far out on the window-sill,
And shook it forth with a royal will.

"Shoot, if you must, this old gray head,
But spare your country's flag," she said.

A shade of sadness, a blush of shame,
Over the face of the leader came;

The nobler nature within him stirred
To life at that woman's deed and word;

"Who touches a hair of yon gray head
Dies like a dog! March on!" he said.

All day long through Frederick street
Sounded the tread of marching feet:

All day long that free flag tost
Over the heads of the rebel host.

Ever its torn folds rose and fell
On the loyal winds that loved it well;

And through the hill-gaps sunset light
Shone over it with a warm good-night.

Barbara Frietchie's work is o'er,
And the Rebel rides on his raids no more.

Honor to her! and let a tear
Fall, for her sake, on Stonewall's bier.

Over Barbara Frietchie's grave,
Flag of Freedom and Union, wave!

Peace and order and beauty draw
Round thy symbol of light and law;

And ever the stars above look down
On thy stars below in Frederick town!.

                    JOHN GREENLEAF WHITTIER [1809-1892]

Anne Rutledge

☆

Out of me unworthy and unknown
The vibrations of deathless music;
'With malice toward none, with charity for all.'
Out of me the forgiveness of millions toward millions,
And the beneficent face of a nation
Shining with justice and truth.

I am Anne Rutledge who sleep beneath these weeds,
Beloved in life of Abraham Lincoln,
Wedded to him, not through union,
But through separation.
Bloom forever, O Republic,
From the dust of my bosom!

EDGAR LEE MASTERS [1869-1950]

Anne Rutledge is a romantic figure of more myth than reality.
Enshrined in folklore as the girl Abraham Lincoln loved and
lost, she seems actually to have been no more than a good friend,
a girl from New Salem, Illinois, who was engaged to an ac-
quaintance of Lincoln's when she died of malarial fever.

The Proclamation

☆

Saint Patrick, slave to Milcho of the herds
Of Ballymena, wakened with these words:
"Arise, and flee
Out from the land of Bondage, and be free!"

Glad as a soul in pain, who hears from heaven
The angels singing of his sins forgiven,

And, wondering, sees
His prison opening to their golden keys,

He rose a man who laid him down a slave,
Shook from his locks the ashes of the grave,
And outward trod
Into the glorious liberty of God.

He cast the symbols of his shame away;
And, passing where the sleeping Milcho lay,
Though back and limb
Smarted with wrong, he prayed, "God pardon him!"

So went he forth; but in God's time he came
To light on Uilline's hills a holy flame;
And, dying, gave
The land a saint that lost him as a slave.

O dark, sad millions, patiently and dumb
Waiting for God, your hour, at last, has come,
And freedom's song
Breaks the long silence of your night of wrong!

Arise and flee! shake off the vile restraint
Of ages; but, like Ballymena's saint,
The oppressor spare,
Heap only on his head the coals of prayer.

Go forth, like him! like him return again,
To bless the land whereon in bitter pain
Ye toiled at first,
And heal with freedom what your slavery cursed.

JOHN GREENLEAF WHITTIER [1807-1892]

Running the Batteries
☆

A moonless night—a friendly one;
A haze dimmed the shadowy shore
As the first lampless boat slid silent on;
Hist! and we spake no more;
We but pointed, and stilly, to what we saw.

We felt the dew, and seemed to feel
The secret like a burden laid.
The first boat melts; and a second keel
Is blent with the foliaged shade—
Their midnight rounds have the rebel officers made?

Unspied as yet. A third—a fourth—
Gunboat and transport in Indian file
Upon the war-path, smooth from the North;
But the watch may they hope to beguile?
The manned river-batteries stretch far mile on mile.

A flame leaps out; they are seen;
Another and another gun roars;
We tell the course of the boats through the screen
By each further fort that pours,
And we guess how they jump from their beds on those
    shrouded shores.

Converging fires. We speak, though low:
"That blastful furnace can they thread?"
"Why, Shadrach, Meshach, and Abednego
Came out all right, we read;
The Lord, be sure, he helps his people, Ned."

How we strain our gaze. On bluffs they shun
A golden growing flame appears—

Confirms to a silvery steadfast one.
"The town is afire!" crows Hugh: "three cheers!"
Lot stops his mouth: "Nay, lad, better three tears."

A purposed light: it shows our fleet;
Yet a little late in its searching ray,
So far and strong that in phantom cheat
Lank on the deck our shadows lay;
The shining flag-ship stings their guns to furious play.

How dread to mark her near the glare
And glade of death the beacon throws
Athwart the racing waters there;
One by one each plainer grows,
Then speeds a blazoned target to our gladdened foes.

The impartial cresset lights as well
The fixed forts to the boats that run;
And, plunged from the ports, their answers swell
Back to each fortress dun;
Ponderous words speaks every monster gun.

Fearless they flash through gates of flame,
The salamanders hard to hit,
Though vivid shows each bulky frame;
And never the batteries intermit,
Nor the boat's huge guns; they fire and flit.

Anon a lull. The beacon dies,
"Are they out of that strait accurst?"
But other flames now dawning rise,
Not mellowly brilliant like the first,
But rolled in smoke, whose whitish volumes burst.

A baleful brand, a hurrying torch
Whereby anew the boats are seen—

A burning transport all alurch!
Breathless we gaze; yet still we glean
Glimpses of beauty as we eager lean.

The effulgence takes an amber glow
Which bathes the hillside villas far;
Affrighted ladies mark the show
Painting the pale magnolia—
The fair, false, Circe light of cruel War.

The barge drifts doomed, a plague-struck one,
Shoreward in yawls the sailors fly.
But the gauntlet now is nearly run,
The spleenful forts by fits reply,
And the burning boat dies down in morning's sky.

All out of range. Adieu, Messieurs!
Jeers, as it speeds, our parting gun.
So burst we through their barriers
And menaces every one;
So Porter proves himself a brave man's son.

HERMAN MELVILLE [1819-1891]

"The Brigade Must Not Know, Sir!"
☆

"Who've ye got there?"—"Only a dying brother,
Hurt in the front just now."
"Good boy! he'll do. Somebody tell his mother
Where he was killed, and how."

"Whom have you there?"—"A crippled courier, Major,
Shot by mistake, we hear.

He was with Stonewall." "Cruel work they've made here;
Quick with him to the rear!"

"Well, who comes next?"—"Doctor, speak low, speak low,
    sir;
Don't let the men find out!
It's Stonewall!"—"God!"—"The brigade must not know, sir,
While there's a foe about!"

Whom have we here—shrouded in martial manner,
Crowned with a martyr's charm?
A grand dead hero, in a living banner,
Born of his heart and arm:

The heart whereon his cause hung—see how clingeth
That banner to his bier!
The arm wherewith his cause struck—hark! how ringeth
His trumpet in their rear!

What have we left? His glorious inspiration,
His prayers in council met.
Living, he laid the first stones of a nation;
And dead, he builds it yet.

ANONYMOUS

O Captain! My Captain!
☆

O Captain! my Captain! our fearful trip is done,
The ship has weather'd every rack, the prize we sought is
    won,
The port is near, the bells I hear, the people all exulting,
While follow eyes the steady keel, the vessel grim and
    daring;

But O heart! heart! heart!
O the bleeding drops of red,
Where on the deck my Captain lies,
Fallen cold and dead.

O Captain! my Captain! rise up and hear the bells;
Rise up—for you the flag is flung—for you the bugle trills,
For you bouquets and ribbon'd wreaths—for you the
    shores a-crowding,
For you they call, the swaying mass, their eager faces
    turning;
Here Captain! dear father!
This arm beneath your head!
It is some dream that on the deck
You've fallen cold and dead.

My Captain does not answer, his lips are pale and still,
My father does not feel my arm, he has no pulse nor will,
The ship is anchor'd safe and sound, its voyage closed and
    done,
From fearful trip the victor ship comes in with object won;
Exult O shores, and ring O bells!
But I with mournful tread,
Walk the deck my Captain lies,
Fallen cold and dead.

WALT WHITMAN [1819-1892]

A NATION GROWS

P ICKING UP the pieces after the war, welding the nation together again, was a long slow process. There was hopeful, superficial optimism of the type reflected in Finch's *The Blue and the Gray*. More common and more accurate was the weary relief to be found in Melville's *The Volunteer to his Rifle*.

But even the pangs of Reconstruction were dulled by the busy, reckless bustling expansion in the air all through the land. Cyrus Field laid a cable to bring immediate communication between Europe and America and this was piously hailed as the beginning of a new understanding among nations that would banish war forever. Alaska, a frozen plot bought from Russia soon after the end of the Civil War, became a goal for romantic adventurers. There were catastrophes like the cave-in at Avondale in 1869 and the Great Chicago Fire of 1871, but America hurried on, swept over and rebuilt.

When Johnny Comes Marching Home
☆

When Johnny comes marching home again,
Hurrah! hurrah!
We'll give him a hearty welcome then,
Hurrah! hurrah!
The men will cheer, the boys will shout,
The ladies, they will all turn out,
And we'll all feel gay,
When Johnny comes marching home.

The old church-bell will peal with joy,
Hurrah! hurrah!
To welcome home our darling boy,
Hurrah! hurrah!
The village lads and lasses say,
With roses they will strew the way;
And we'll all feel gay,
When Johnny comes marching home.

Get ready for the jubilee,
Hurrah! hurrah!
We'll give the hero three times three,
Hurrah! hurrah!
The laurel-wreath is ready now
To place upon his loyal brow,
And we'll all feel gay,
When Johnny comes marching home.

Let love and friendship on that day,
Hurrah! hurrah!
Their choicest treasures then display,
Hurrah! hurrah!
And let each one perform some part,

To fill with joy the warrior's heart;
And we'll all feel gay,
When Johnny comes marching home.

PATRICK SARSFIELD GILMORE [1829-1892]

Ku-Klux
☆

We have sent him seeds of the melon's core,
And nailed a warning upon his door;
By the Ku-Klux laws we can do no more.

Down in the hollow, 'mid crib and stack,
The roof of his low-porched house looms black,
Not a line of light at the doorsill's crack.

Yet arm and mount! and mask and ride!
The hounds can sense though the fox may hide!
And for a word too much men oft have died.

The clouds blow heavy towards the moon.
The edge of the storm will reach it soon.
The kildee cries and the lonesome loon.

In the pause of the thunder rolling low,
A rifle's answer—who shall know
From the wind's fierce hurl and the rain's black blow?

Only the signature written grim
At the end of the message brought to him—
A hempen rope and a twisted limb.

So arm and mount! and mask and ride!
The hounds can sense though the fox may hide!
And for a word too much men oft have died.

MADISON CAWEIN [1865-1914]

The Ku Klux Klan was formed in Pulaski, Tennessee in 1866 as
a secret organization to combat Northern carpetbaggers, newly
freed Negroes and others considered political enemies. There
may have been some traces of idealism in its original member-
ship, although it followed from the first a pattern of extra-legal
violence including whippings and lynchings. The original Klan
dissolved in 1869, but its pattern of violence remained and the
name was revived in 1915 to grace an anti-Catholic, anti-Semitic,
anti-Negro organization which continues to exist in some areas
today.

The Rebel
☆

Oh, I'm a good old rebel, that's what I am,
And for this land of freedom, I don't give a damn;
I'm glad I fought agin her, I only wish we'd won,
And I ain't axed any pardon for anything I've done.

I fought with old Bob Lee for three years about,
Got wounded in four places and starved at Point Lookout.
I caught the rheumatism a-campin' in the snow,
And I killed a chance of Yankees and I wish I'd killed
    some mo'!

Three hundred thousand Yankees is dead in Southern dust,
We got three hundred thousand before they conquered us;
They died of Southern fever, of Southern steel and shot—
I wish they was three million instead of what we got.

I hate the Constitution, this great republic, too;
I hate the nasty eagle, and the uniform so blue;
I hate their glorious banner, and all their flags and fuss.
Those lying, thieving Yankees, I hate 'em wuss and wuss.

I hate the Yankee nation and everything they do;
I hate the Declaration of Independence too;
I hate the glorious Union, 'tis dripping with our blood;
I hate the striped banner, I fought it all I could.

I won't be reconstructed! I'm better now than them;
And for a carpetbagger, I don't give a damn;
So I'm off for the frontier, soon as I can go,
I'll prepare me a weapon and start for Mexico.

I can't take up my musket and fight them now no mo',
But I'm not goin' to love 'em, and that is certain sho';
And I don't want no pardon for what I was or am,
I won't be reconstructed and I don't give a damn.

INNES RANDOLPH

The Blue and the Gray
☆

By the flow of the inland river,
Whence the fleets of iron have fled,
Where the blades of the grave-grass quiver,
Asleep are the ranks of the dead:
Under the sod and the dew,
Waiting the judgment-day;
Under the one, the Blue,
Under the other, the Gray.

These in the robings of glory,
Those in the gloom of defeat,
All with the battle-blood gory,
In the dusk of eternity meet:
Under the sod and the dew,
Waiting the judgment-day;
Under the laurel, the Blue,
Under the willow, the Gray.

. . . .

So, when the summer calleth,
On forest and field of grain,
With an equal murmur falleth
The cooling drip of the rain:
Under the sod and the dew,
Waiting the judgment-day;
Wet with the rain, the Blue,
Wet with the rain, the Gray.

. . . .

No more shall the war-cry sever,
Or the winding rivers be red;
They banish our anger forever
When they laurel the graves of our dead!
Under the sod and the dew,
Waiting the judgment-day;
Love and tears for the Blue,
Tears and love for the Gray.

FRANCIS MILES FINCH [1827-1907]

The Returned Volunteer to His Rifle
☆

Over this hearth—my father's seat—
Repose, to patriot-memory dear,
Thou tried companion, whom at last I greet

By steepy banks of Hudson here.
How oft I told thee of this scene—
The Highlands blue—the river's narrowing sheen.
Little at Gettysburg we thought
To find such haven; but God kept it green.
Long rest! with belt, and bayonet, and canteen.

HERMAN MELVILLE [1819-1891]

The Cable Hymn
☆

O lonely bay of Trinity,
O dreary shores, give ear!
Lean down, unto the white-lipped sea
The voice of God to hear!

From world to world His couriers fly,
Thought-winged and shod with fire;
The angel of His stormy sky
Rides down the sunken wire.

What saith the herald of the Lord?
"The world's long strife is done;
Close wedded by that mystic cord,
Its continents are one.

"And one in heart, as one in blood,
Shall all her peoples be;
The hands of human brotherhood
Are clasped beneath the sun.

"Through Orient seas, o'er Afric's plain
And Asian mountains borne,

The vigor of the Northern brain
Shall nerve the world outworn.

"From clime to clime, from shore to shore,
Shall thrill the magic thread;
The new Prometheus steals once more
The fire that wakes the dead."

Throb on, strong pulse of thunder! beat
From answering beach to beach;
Fuse nations in thy kindly heat,
And melt the chains of each!

Wild terror of the sky above,
Glide tamed and dumb below!
Bear gently, Ocean's carrier-dove,
Thy errands to and fro.

Weave on, swift shuttle of the Lord,
Beneath the deep so far,
The bridal robe of earth's accord,
The funeral shroud of war!

For lo! the fall of Ocean's wall
Space mocked and time outrun;
And round the world the thought of all
Is as the thought of one!

The poles unite, the zones agree,
The tongues of striving cease;
As on the Sea of Galilee
The Christ is whispering, Peace!

JOHN GREENLEAF WHITTIER [1807-1892]

Alaska
☆

Ice built, ice bound, and ice bounded,
Such cold seas of silence! such room!
Such snow-light, such sea-light, confounded
With thunders that smite like a doom!
Such grandeur! such glory! such gloom!
Hear that boom! Hear that deep distant boom
Of an avalanche hurled
Down this unfinished world!

Ice seas! and ice summits! ice spaces
In splendor of white, as God's throne!
Ice worlds to the pole! and ice places
Untracked, and unnamed, and unknown!
Hear that boom! Hear the grinding, the groan
Of the ice-gods in pain! Hear the moan
Of yon ice mountain hurled
Down this unfinished world!

JOAQUIN MILLER [1839-1913]

The Avondale Mine Disaster
☆

Good Christians all, both great and small, I pray you lend
    an ear,
And listen with attention while the truth I do declare,
When you hear this lamentation, it will cause you to turn
    pale—
All about the suffocation in the mines of Avondale.

On the sixteenth day of September, in eighteen sixty-nine,
Those miners all, they got a call to go work in the mine;

But little did they think that death would gloom their vale
Before they would return again from the mines of
    Avondale.

The women, and the children, too, their hearts were filled
    with joy
To see their men go work again, and likewise every boy;
But a dismal sight, in broad daylight, which made them
    soon turn pale,
When they saw the breakers burning in the mines of
    Avondale.

From here and there and everywhere they gathered in a
    crowd,
Some tearing off their clothes and hair, and crying out
    aloud:
"Get out our husbands and our sons, for death is going to
    steal
Their lives away, without delay, in the mines of
    Avondale!"

But all in vain! there was no hope one single soul to save;
There was no second outlet to this ignominious cave.
No pen can write the awful fright, and horror did prevail
Among those dying victims in the mines of Avondale.

A consultation then took place; some were asked to
    volunteer
For to go down this dismal shaft to seek their comrades
    dear.
Two Welshmen brave, without dismay and courage
    without fail,
Went down the shafts without delay, in the mines of
    Avondale.

When at the bottom they arrived, and thought to make
    their way,
One of them died for the want of air, while the other in
    great dismay—
He gave a sign to lift him up, to tell the fearful tale,
That all were lost forever in the mines of Avondale.

A second effort then took place, to send down some fresh
    air.
The next men that went down again, they took of them
    great care.
They traversed then the chambers, and this time did not
    fail
In finding their dead bodies in the mines of Avondale.

Sixty-seven was the number that in one heap were found.
They seemed to be awaiting their sad fate underground.
They found a father with his son clasped in his arms so
    frail;
There were heart-rending scenes there in the mines of
    Avondale.

Now to conclude and make an end, the number to pen
    down,
One hundred and ten of brave, stout men were smothered
    underground.
There in their grave till their last day; their widows weep
    and wail,
And oft-rent cries may rend the skies all around through
    Avondale.

ANONYMOUS

Chicago
☆

Blackened and bleeding, helpless, panting, prone,
On the charred fragments of her shattered throne
Lies she who stood but yesterday alone.
Queen of the West! by some enchanter taught
To lift the glory of Aladdin's court,
Then lose the spell that all that wonder wrought.

Like her own prairies by some chance seed sown,
Like her own prairies in one brief day grown,
Like her own prairies in one fierce night mown.

She lifts her voice, and in her pleading call
We hear the cry of Macedon to Paul,
The cry for help that makes her kin to all.

But haply with wan fingers may she feel
The silver cup hid in the proffered meal,
The gifts her kinship and our loves reveal.

BRET HARTE [1836-1902]

★★★★★★★

There were still the Indians. They succeeded in massacring General George Custer and his band at the Little Big Horn in 1876. We could still think them odd and savage for resisting the "civilized" encroachment that had turned their prairies and forests, their hunting grounds, into something unimaginable in the wildest prophecies of a medicine man a hundred years before.

Custer's Last Charge
☆

DEAD! Is it possible? He, the bold rider,
Custer, our hero, the first in the fight,
Charming the bullets of yore to fly wider,
Far from our battle-king's ringlets of light!
Dead, our young chieftain, and dead, all forsaken!
No one to tell us the way of his fall!
Slain in the desert, and never to waken,
Never, not even to victory's call!

Proud for his fame that last day that he met them!
All the night long he had been on their track,
Scorning their traps and the men that had set them,
Wild for a charge that should never give back.
There on the hilltop he halted and saw them,—
Lodges all loosened and ready to fly;
Hurrying scouts with the tidings to awe them,
Told of his coming before he was nigh.

All the wide valley was full of their forces,
Gathered to cover the lodges' retreat!—
Warriors running in haste to their horses,
Thousands of enemies close to his feet!
Down in the valleys the ages had hollowed,
There lay the Sitting Bull's camp for a prey!
Numbers! What recked he? What recked those who
        followed—
Men who had fought ten to one ere that day?

Out swept the squadrons, the fated three hundred,
Into the battle-line steady and full;
Then down the hillside exultingly thundered,
Into the hordes of the old Sitting Bull!

Wild Ogalallah, Arapahoe, Cheyenne,
Wild Horse's braves, and the rest of their crew,
Shrank from that charge like a herd from a lion,—
Then closed around, the grim horde of wild Sioux!

Right to their centre he charged, and then facing—
Hark to those yells! and around them, O see!
Over the hilltops the Indians came racing,
Coming as fast as the waves of the sea!
Red was the circle of fire around them;
No hope of victory, no ray of light,
Shot through that terrible black cloud without them,
Brooding in death over Custer's last fight.

Then did he blench? Did he die like a craven,
Begging those torturing fiends for his life?
Was there a soldier who carried the Seven,
Flinched like a coward or fled from the strife?
No, by the blood of our Custer, no quailing!
There in the midst of the Indians they close,
Hemmed in by thousands, but ever assailing,
Fighting like tigers, all 'bayed amid foes!

Thicker and thicker the bullets came singing;
Down go the horses and riders and all;
Swiftly the warriors round them were ringing,
Circling like buzzards awaiting their fall.
See the wild steeds of the mountain and prairie,
Savage eyes gleaming from forests of mane;
Quivering lances with pennons so airy,
War-painted warriors charging amain.

Backward, again and again, they were driven,
Shrinking to close with the lost little band;
Never a cap that had worn the bright Seven

Bowed till its wearer was dead on the strand.
Closer and closer the death circle growing,
Ever the leader's voice, clarion clear,
Rang out his words of encouragement glowing,
"We can but die once, boys,—we'll sell our lives dear!"

Dearly they sold them like Berserkers raging,
Facing the death that encircled them round;
Death's bitter pangs by their vengeance assuaging,
Marking their tracks by their dead on the ground,
Comrades, our children shall yet tell their story,—
Custer's last charge on the old Sitting Bull;
And ages shall swear that the cup of his glory
Needed but that death to render it full.

FREDERICK WHITTAKER [1838-1917]

★★★★★★★

More soldiers, luckier and cannier than Custer, avenged
his massacre, but what really destroyed the Indians was
the railroad. Railroads spanned the whole country now,
and brought the centers of civilization so close together
that no aborigine could hold out. We were proud of the
railroads and only a rare independent soul like Thoreau
could disdain them. We made a folk hero out of an en-
gineer, Casey Jones.

What's the Railroad
☆

What's the railroad to me?
I never go to see
Where it ends.
It fills a few hollows,
And makes banks for the swallows,
It sets the sand a-blowing,
And the blackberries a-growing.

HENRY DAVID THOREAU [1817-1862]

Casey Jones
☆

Come all you rounders if you want to hear
The story of a brave engineer;
Casey Jones was the hogger's name,
On a big eight-wheeler, boys, he won his fame.
Caller called Casey at half-past four,
He kissed his wife at the station door,
Mounted to the cabin with orders in his hand,
And took his farewell trip to the promised land.

Casey Jones, he mounted to the cabin,
Casey Jones, with his orders in his hand!
Casey Jones, he mounted to the cabin,
Took his farewell trip into the promised land.

Put in your water and shovel in your coal,
Put your head out the window, watch the drivers roll,
I'll run her open till she leaves the rail,
'Cause we're eight hours late with the Western Mail!
He looked at his watch and his watch was slow,
Looked at the water and the water was low,
Turned to his fireboy and then he said,
"We'll get to 'Frisco, but we'll all be dead!"

[CHORUS]

Casey pulled up old Reno Hill,
Tooted for the crossing with an awful shrill,
Snakes all knew by the engine's moans
That the hogger at the throttle was Casey Jones.
He pulled up short two miles from the place,
Number Four stared him right in the face,
Turned to his fireboy, said "You'd better jump,
'Cause there's two locomotives that're going to bump!"

[CHORUS]

Casey said, just before he died,
"There's two more roads I'd like to ride."
Fireboy said, "What can they be?"
"The Rio Grande and the Old S.P."
Mrs. Jones sat on her bed a-sighing,
Got a telegram that Casey was dying,
Said, "Go to bed, children; hush your crying,
'Cause you've got another papa on the Salt Lake Line."

ANONYMOUS

★★★★★★★

We spun songs out of villains as well as heroes. Charles
Guiteau, the unbalanced office-seeker who shot Presi-
dent Garfield in 1881, was turned into a ballad along
with such good-bad figures as Billy the Kid and Jesse
James.

Garfield's Murder
☆

Come all ye tender-hearted people,
And listen to what I say.
And likewise pay attention
To these few words from me.
For the murder of James A. Garfield
I am condemned to die,
On the 30th day of June
I meet my fatal doom.

[CHORUS]

My name is Charles Guiteau,
That I cannot deny,
And I leave my aged parents
In sorrow for to die.
How little did they think
While in my youthful bloom,
I'd be taken to the scaffold
To meet my fatal doom.

I was down at the depot,
I tried to make my escape,
But Providence being against me
I found it was too late.
I was taken to the prison,
All in my youthful bloom,
And today I take the scaffold,
To meet my fatal doom.

[CHORUS]

I tried to play insane,
But found that would not do.
The people being against me,
They proved my sentence true.
Judge Cox he read my sentence,
The clerk he wrote it down,
And on the 30th day of June
I meet my fatal doom.

[CHORUS]

My sister came to the prison
To bid her last farewell;

She threw her arms around me
And wept most bitterly,
Saying, "My dearest, darling brother,
You are condemned to die
For the murder of James A. Garfield,
Upon the scaffold high."

[CHORUS]

ANONYMOUS

Billy the Kid
☆

I'll sing you a true song of Billy the Kid,
I'll sing of the desperate deeds that he did
Way out in New Mexico long, long ago,
When a man's only chance was his own forty-four.

When Billy the Kid was a very young lad,
In old Silver City he went to the bad;
Way out in the West with a gun in his hand
At the age of twelve years he killed his first man.

Fair Mexican maidens play guitars and sing
A song about Billy, their boy bandit king,
How ere his young manhood had reached its sad end
He'd a notch on his pistol for twenty-one men.

'Twas on the same night when poor Billy died
He said to his friends: "I am not satisfied;
There are twenty-one men I have put bullets through
And Sheriff Pat Garrett must make twenty-two."

Now this is how Billy the Kid met his fate:
The bright moon was shining, the hour it was late.
Shot down by Pat Garrett, who once was his friend,
The young outlaw's life had now come to its end.

There's many a man with a face fine and fair
Who starts out in life with a chance to be square,
But just like poor Billy he wanders astray
And loses his life in the very same way.

ANONYMOUS

Jesse James
☆

Jesse James was a two-gun man,
(*Roll on, Missouri!*)
Strong-arm chief of an outlaw clan
(*From Kansas to Illinois!*)
He twirled an old Colt forty-five,
(*Roll on, Missouri!*)
They never took Jesse James alive.
(*Roll, Missouri, roll!*)
Jesse James was King of the Wes';
(*Cataracks in the Missouri!*)
He'd a di'mon' heart in his lef' bres';
(*Brown Missouri rolls!*)
He'd a fire in his heart no hurt could stifle;
(*Thunder, Missouri!*)
Lion eyes an' a Winchester rifle.
(*Missouri, roll down!*)

Jesse James rode a pinto hawse;
Come at night to a water-cawse;

Tetched with the rowel that pinto's flank;
She sprung the torrent from bank to bank.

Jesse rode through a sleepin' town;
Looked the moonlit street both up an' down;
Crack-crack-crack, the street ran flames
An' a great voice cried, "I'm Jesse James!"

Hawse an' afoot they're after Jess!
(*Roll on, Missouri!*)
Spurrin' and spurrin'—but he's gone Wes'.
(*Brown Missouri rolls!*)
He was ten foot tall when he stood in his boots;
(*Lightnin' light the Missouri!*)
More'n a match fer sich galoots.
(*Roll, Missouri, roll!*)

Jesse James rode outa the sage;
Roun' the rocks come the swayin' stage;
Straddlin' the road a giant stan's
An' a great voice bellers, "Throw up yer han's!"

Jesse raked in the di'mon' rings,
The big gold watches an' the yuther things;
Jesse divvied 'em then an' thar
With a cryin' child had lost her mar.

The U.S. Troopers is after Jess;
(*Roll on, Missouri!*)
Their hawses sweat foam, but he's gone Wes';
(*Hear Missouri roar!*)
He was broad as a b'ar, he'd a ches' like a drum,
(*Wind an' rain through Missouri!*)
An' his red hair flamed like Kingdom Come.
(*Missouri down to the sea!*)

Jesse James all alone in the rain
Stopped an' stuck up the Eas'-boun' train;
Swayed through the coaches with horns an' a tail,
Lit out with the bullion an' the registered mail.

Jess made 'em all turn green with fright,
Quakin' in the aisles in the pitch-black night;
An' he give all the bullion to a pore ole tramp
Campin' nigh the cuttin' in the dirt an' damp.

The whole U.S. is after Jess;
(*Roll on, Missouri!*)
The son-of-a-gun, if he ain't gon Wes';
(*Missouri to the sea!*)
He could chew cold iron an' spit blue flame;
(*Cataracks down the Missouri!*)
He rode on a catamount he'd larned to tame.
(*Hear that Missouri roll!*)

Jesse James rode into a bank;
Give his pinto a tetch on the flank;
Jumped the teller's window with an awful crash;
Heaved up the safe an' twirled his mustache;

He said, "So long, boys!" he yelped, "So long!
Feelin' porely today— I ain't feelin' strong!"
Rode right through the wall agoin' crack-crack-crack—
Took the safe home to Mother in a gunny-sack.

They're creepin', they're crawlin', they're stalkin' Jess;
(*Roll on, Missouri!*)
They's a rumor he's gone much further Wes';
(*Roll, Missouri, roll*)
They's word of a cayuse hitched to the bars

(*Ruddy clouds on Missouri!*)
Of a golden sunset that bursts into stars.
(*Missouri, roll down!*)

Jesse James rode hell fer leather;
He was a hawse an' a man together;
In a cave in a mountain high up in air
He lived with a rattlesnake, a wolf, an' a bear.

Jesse's heart was as sof' as a woman;
Fer guts an' stren'th he was sooper-human;
He could put six shots through a woodpecker's eye
And take in one swaller a gallon o' rye.

They sought him here an' they sought him there,
(*Roll on, Missouri!*)
But he strides by night through the ways of the air,
(*Brown Missouri rolls!*)
They say he was took an' they say he is dead;
(*Thunder, Missouri!*)
But he ain't—he's a sunset overhead!
(*Missouri down to the sea!*)

Jesse James was a Hercules.
When he went through the woods he tore up the trees.
When he went on the plains he smoked the groun'
An' the hull lan' shuddered fer miles aroun',

Jesse James wore a red bandanner
That waved on the breeze like the Star Spangled Banner;
In seven states he cut up dadoes.
He's gone with the buffler an' the desperadoes.

Yes, Jesse James was a two-gun man
(*Roll on, Missouri!*)

The same as when this song began;
(*From Kansas to Illinois!*)
An' when you see a sunset burst into flames
(*Lightnin' light the Missouri!*)
Or a thunderstorm blaze—that's Jesse James!
(*Hear that Missouri roll!*)

WILLIAM ROSE BENÉT [1886-1950]

★★★★★★★

River and lake traffic still competed with the rails and
most Americans could tap their feet to the chanty of
Dance the Boatman. The Indians might be almost gone,
but the West was wild and woolly still, and disillusion-
ing for dream-laden tenderfeet like the boys cajoled
into contracts by the Buffalo Skinners.

Dance the Boatman
☆

The boatman he can dance and sing
And he's the lad for any old thing.
   Dance the boatman, dance!
   Dance the boatman, dance!
He'll dance all night on his toes so light
And go down to his boat in the morning.
   Hooraw the boatman, ho!
   Spends his money with the gals ashore!
   Hooraw the boatman, ho!
   Rolling down the Ohio!

From Louisville down the Ohio,
He's known wherever them boats do go,
  Dance the boatman, dance!
  Dance the boatman, dance!
He'll drink and dance and kiss them all,
And away in his boat in the morning.
  Hooraw the boatman, ho!
  Spends his money with the girls ashore!
  Hooraw the boatman, ho!
  Rolling down the Ohio!

The girls all wait for boatman Bill,
For he's the one they all love still,
  Dance the boatman, dance!
  Dance the boatman, dance!
He'll buy them drinks and swing them high,
And leave in his boat in the morning.
  Hooraw the boatman, ho!
  Spends his money with the gals ashore!
  Hooraw the boatman, ho!
  Rolling down the Ohio!

ANONYMOUS

The Buffalo Skinners
☆

Come all you jolly buffalo skinners and listen to my song,
If you will pay attention I won't detain you long.
'Tis concerning some jolly bull-skinners that did agree to
    go
And spend a summer pleasantly on the Range of the
    Buffalo.

It was in the town of Jacksboro in the spring of seventy-
    three
That a man by the name of Crigor came walking up to
    me;
Says he, "How do you do, young fellow, and how would
    you like to go
And spend a summer pleasantly on the Range of the
    Buffalo?"

On being out of employment, I answered unto him,
"Going out with you on the Buffalo Range depends upon
    the pay.
If you will pay good wages and transportation too,
I will go with you to the Buffalo Range and spend a
    month or two."

"Oh yes, I'll pay good wages and transportation too,
If you will go with me to the Buffalo Range and spend the
    summer through;
But if you get tired and homesick and to Jacksboro go,
I will not pay you wages from the Range of the Buffalo."

By such talk and flatteration he enlisted quite a crew, I
    think 'twas twenty-one.
And when he got to Peas River our troubles then begun.
The very first tail I tried to split—Cripes! How I cut my
    thumb!
And out skinning those damned old stinkers, our lives we
    had no show,
For the Indians watched to pick us off out skinning the
    buffalo.

We lived on rotten buffalo hump and damned old iron-
    wedge bread,
Strong coffee, croton water to drink, and a bull hide for a
    bed;

And the way the gray-back worked on us, God knows it
    was not slow!
God grant there is no hell on earth like the Range of the
    Buffalo!

The season being ended, Old Crigor could not pay—
The outfit was so extravagant he was in debt that day—
But among us jolly bull-skinners bankruptcy would not go,
So we left poor Crigor's bones to bleach on the Range of
    the Buffalo.

Now we are 'cross the Brazos River and homeward we are
    bound,
And in this hell-fired country we never shall be found.
We will go home to our wives and sweethearts and tell
    others not to go
To that God-forsaken hell on earth—the Range of the
    Buffalo.

ANONYMOUS

★★★★★★★

And now another war, part of our boisterous growing-up.
Cuba, just a step from Florida, had long been unhappy
under the rule of Spain. Free Cuban forces seemed at last
within sight of throwing off Spanish rule and the United
States, although officially neutral, was sympathetic to
the Cuban rebels. The unexplained explosion of the
United States battleship *Maine* in Havana harbor in
1898 led to a declaration of war against Spain some two
months later.

The United States had remained aloof from foreign struggles since 1812. Now, for the first time in almost a hundred years, we were at war with a nation classed as a great power. But Spain had suffered attrition over the years. At Manila in the Philippines, Admiral Dewey destroyed the Spanish Pacific fleet in one day. In Cuba, the American force made short work of the Spanish opposition and suffered most of its casualties from disease and poor administration. Stephen Crane, a young writer covering the war as a correspondent, could describe heroism movingly when he saw it, but most of what he saw confirmed his bitter view of war as waste.

The victory over Spain fixed the status of the United States as a major world power on land and sea. The less pleasant result, a long campaign in the Philippines to put down a rebellion of the very natives we had pledged ourselves to free, brought searching second thoughts, like Moody's, about power and expansion.

Cuba Libre
☆

Comes a cry from Cuban water—
From the warm, dusk Antilles—
From the lost Atlanta's daughter,
Drowned in blood as drowned in seas;
Comes a cry of purpled anguish—
See her struggles, hear her cries!
Shall she live, or shall she languish?
Shall she sink, or shall she rise?

She shall rise, by all that's holy!
She shall live and she shall last;

Rise as we, when crushed and lowly,
From the blackness of the past.
Bid her strike! Lo, it is written
Blood for blood and life for life.
Bid her smite, as she is smitten;
Stars and stripes were born of strife.

Once we flashed her lights of freedom,
Lights that dazzled her dark eyes
Till she could but yearning heed them,
Reach her hands and try to rise.
Then they stabbed her, choked her, drowned **her**
Till we scarce could hear a note.
Ah! these rusting chains that bound her!
Oh! these robbers at her throat!

And the kind who forged these fetters?
Ask five hundred years for news.
Stake and thumbscrew for their betters!
Inquisitions! Banished Jews!
Chains and slavery! What reminder
Of one red man in that land?
Why, these very chains that bind her
Bound Columbus, foot and hand!

Shall she rise as rose Columbus,
From his chains, from shame and wrong—
Rise as Morning, matchless, wondrous—
Rise as some rich morning song—
Rise a ringing song and story,
Valor, Love personified?
Stars and stripes espouse her glory,
Love and Liberty allied.

JOAQUIN MILLER [1839-1913]

War Is Kind
☆

Do not weep, maiden, for war is kind.
Because your lover threw wild hands toward the sky
Do not weep.
War is kind.

Hoarse, booming drums of the regiment,
Little souls who thirst for fight,
These men were born to drill and die.
The unexplained glory flies above them,
Great is the battle-god, great, and his kingdom—
A field where a thousand corpses lie.

Do not weep, babe, for war is kind.
Because your father tumbled in the yellow trenches
Raged at his breast, gulped and died,
Do not weep.
War is kind.

Swift blazing flag of the regiment,
Eagle with crest of red and gold,
These men were born to drill and die.
Point for them the virtue of slaughter,
Make plain to them the excellence of killing
And a field where a thousand corpses lie.

Mother whose heart hung humble as a button
On the bright splendid shroud of your son,
Do not weep.
War is kind.

STEPHEN CRANE [1871-1900]

Stephen Crane had written one of the greatest war (and anti-war) novels of our literature in *The Red Badge of Courage* without ever having observed war at first hand. When he served as a correspondent covering the Spanish-American War, first-hand experience served only to confirm his view of war as waste, and he restated this belief in the poem above and in other verse which etched in irony the human love of investing horror with glory.

On a Soldier Fallen in the Philippines

☆

Streets of the roaring town,
Hush for him, hush, be still!
He comes, who was stricken down
Doing the word of our will.
Hush! Let him have his state.
Give him his soldier's crown,
The grists of trade can wait
Their grinding at the mill,
But he cannot wait for his honor, now the trumpet has
    been blown.
Wreathe pride now for his granite brow, lay love on his
    breast of stone.

Toll! Let the great bells toll
Till the clashing air is dim,
Did we wrong this parted soul?
We will make it up to him.
Toll! Let him never guess
What work we set him to.
Laurel, laurel, yes;
He did what we bade him do.
Praise, and never a whispered hint but the fight he fought
    was good;

Never a word that the blood on his sword was his
    country's own heart's blood.

A flag for the soldier's bier
Who dies that this land may live;
Oh, banners, banners here,
That he doubt not nor misgive!
That he heed not from the tomb
The evil days draw near
When the nation, robed in gloom,
With its faithless part shall strive.
Let him never dream that his bullet's scream went wide
    of its island mark,
Home to the heart of his shining land where she stumbled
    and sinned in the dark.

              WILLIAM VAUGHN MOODY [1869-1910]

★★★★★★★

Sober thoughtfulness like Moody's didn't cast much of a
pall over our continuing expansion. A young man named
Alfred Damon Runyon, very far from the Times Square
he was later to make his own literary property, marveled
at the building of the Panama Canal in 1908. We were
still building, moving, pushing back frontiers across the
land. John Henry and his duel with a steam-hammer be-
came part of our story, and there were still cowboys who
rode the plains of the West and boll weevils that plagued
cotton growers in the south. All this expansion had be-
gun to have an effect upon the working-man at its base.

The Industrial Workers of the World, nicknamed "Wob-blies," held meetings to press for wider-ranging, stronger labor unions. The almost legendary Joe Hill put union words to old evangelistic tunes to spread the Wobbly message.

A Song of Panama
☆

"Chuff! chuff! chuff!" An' a mountainbluff
Is moved by the shovel's song;
"Chuff! chuff! chuff!" Oh, the grade is rough
A liftin' the landscape along!

We are ants upon a mountain, but we're leavin' of our
    dent,
An' our teeth-marks bitin' scenery they will show the way
    we went;
We're a liftin' half creation, an' we're chargin' it around,
Just to suit our playful purpose when we're diggin' in the
    ground.

"Chuff! chuff! chuff!" Oh, the grade is rough,
An' the way to the sea is long;
"Chuff! chuff! chuff!" an' the engines puff
In tune to the shovel's song!

We're a shiftin' miles like inches, and we grab a forest here
Just to switch it over yonder so's to leave an angle clear;
We're a pushin' leagues o' swamps aside so's we can hurry
    by—
An' if we had to do it we would probably switch the sky!

"Chuff! chuff! chuff!" Oh, it's hard enough
When you're changin' a job wrong;
"Chuff! chuff! chuff!" an' there's no rebuff
To the shovel a singin' its song!

You hears it in the mornin' an' you hears it late at night—
It's our battery keepin' action with support o' dynamite;
Oh, you gets it for your dinner, an' the scenery skips along
In a movin' panorama to the chargin' shovel's song!

"Chuff! chuff! chuff!" an' it grabs the scruff
Of a hill an' boosts it along;
"Chuff! chuff! chuff!" Oh, the grade is rough,
But it gives to the shovel's song!

This is a fight that's fightin', an' the battle's to the death;
There ain't no stoppin' here to rest or even catch your
      breath;
You ain't no noble hero, an' you leave no gallant name—
You're fightin' Nature's army, an' it ain't no easy game!

"Chuff! chuff! chuff!" Oh, the grade is rough,
An' the way to the end is long,
"Chuff! chuff! chuff!" an' the engines puff
As we lift the landscape along!

ALFRED DAMON RUNYON [1884-1946]

John Henry
☆

When John Henry was a little boy,
Sitting upon his father's knee,
His father said, "Look here, my boy,

You must be a steel driving man like me,
You must be a steel driving man like me."

John Henry went up on the mountain,
Just to drive himself some steel.
The rocks was so tall and John Henry so small,
He said lay down hammer and squeal,
He said lay down hammer and squeal.

John Henry had a little wife,
And the dress she wore was red;
The last thing before he died,
He said, "Be true to me when I'm dead,
Oh, be true to me when I'm dead."

John Henry's wife ask him for fifteen cents,
And he said he didn't have but a dime,
Said, "If you wait till the rising sun goes down,
I'll borrow it from the man in the mine,
I'll borrow it from the man in the mine."

John Henry started on the right-hand side,
And the steam drill started on the left.
He said, "Before I'd let that steam drill beat me
    down,
I'd hammer my fool self to death,
Oh, I'd hammer my fool self to death."

The steam drill started at half-past six,
John Henry started the same time.
John Henry struck bottom at half-past eight,
And the steam drill didn't bottom till nine,
And the steam drill didn't bottom till nine.

John Henry said to his captain,

"A man, he ain't nothing but a man,
Before I'd let that steam drill beat me down,
I'd die with the hammer in my hand,
Oh, I'd die with the hammer in my hand."

John Henry said to his shaker,
"Shaker, why don't you sing just a few more rounds?
And before the setting sun goes down,
You're gonna hear this hammer of mine sound,
You're gonna hear this hammer of mine sound."

John Henry hammered on the mountain,
He hammered till half-past three,
He said, "This big Bend Tunnel on the C. & O. road
Is going to be the death of me,
Lord! is going to be the death of me."

John Henry had a little baby boy,
You could hold him in the palm of your hand.
The last words before he died,
"Son, you must be a steel driving man,
Son, you must be a steel driving man."

John Henry had a little woman,
And the dress she wore was red,
She went down the railroad track and never come back,
Said she was going where John Henry fell dead,
Said she was going where John Henry fell dead.

John Henry hammering on the mountain,
As the whistle blew for half-past two,
The last word I heard him say,
"Captain, I've hammered my insides in two,
Lord, I've hammered my insides in two."

ANONYMOUS

Cowboy's Lament
☆

As I was a-walking the streets of Laredo,
As I was a-walking, quite early one morn,
I spied a young cowboy all dressed in his buckskins,
All dressed in his buckskins, all fit for his grave.

"Then beat the drum lowly and play the fife slowly,
Beat up the death marches as they carry me along;
Take me to the prairie and fire a volley o'er me,
For I'm a young cowboy and dying alone.

"Once in my saddle I used to go dashing,
Once in my saddle I used to ride gay;
But I just took up drinking and then to card-playing,
Got shot by a gambler, and dying to-day.

"Go gather around me a lot of wild cowboys,
And tell them the story of a comrade's sad fate;
Warn them quite gently to give up wild roving,
To give up wild roving before it's too late.

"Some one write to my gray-headed mother,
And then to my sister, my sister so dear;
There is another far dearer than mother,
Who would bitterly weep if she knew I were here.

"O bury beside me my knife and my shooter,
My spurs on my heels, my rifle by my side;
Over my coffin put a bottle of brandy,
That the cowboys may drink as they carry me along.

"Some one go bring me a drink of cold water,
(A drink of cold water," the poor fellow said;)

As they turned the soul had departed,
He had gone on a round-up and the cowboy was dead.

ANONYMOUS

The Ballad of the Boll Weevil
☆

First time I saw little Weevil he was on the western plain,
Next time I saw him he was riding a Memphis train.
He was seeking him a home, a happy home.

Next time I saw him he was settin' on a cotton square.
The next time I saw him he had his family there.
He was seeking him a home, a happy home.

Next time I saw him he was runnin' a spinnin' wheel;
The next time I saw him he was ridin' in an automobile.
He was seeking him a home, a happy home.

Mr. Merchant said to the farmer, "Well what do you think
    of that?
If you'll get rid of little Weevil, I'll give you a Stetson
    hat."
He's seeking him a home, a happy home.

Mr. Farmer took little Weevil and put him in Paris green.
"Thank you, Mr. Farmer; it's the best I ever seen.
I'm going to have a home, a happy home."

Then he took little Weevil, put him in a block of ice.
"Thank you, Mr. Farmer; it's so cool and nice.
I'm going to have a home, a happy home."

Mr. Farmer then got angry and sent him up in a balloon.
"Good-bye, Mr. Farmer; I'll see you again next June.
I'll be seeking me a home, a happy home."

Little Weevil took Mr. Farmer, throwed him in the sand,
Put on Mr. Farmer's overcoat, stood up like a natural man.
"I'm going to have a home, a happy home."

Little Weevil said to the sharpshooter, "Better get up on
    your feet.
Look down across the Delta at the cotton we'll have to
    reap.
We've got us a home, a happy home."

Mr. Merchant said to the farmer, "I can not see your
    route.
Got a mortgate on old Beck and Kate; just as well be
    taking them out.
And bring them home, and bring them home."

Come on, old woman, and we will travel out West,
The weevils et up everything we've got but your old
    cotton dress.
And it's full of holes, it's full of holes."

ANONYMOUS

There Is Power in a Union
☆

Would you have Freedom from wage-slavery?
    Then join in the Grand Industrial Band.
Would you from misery and hunger be free?
    Then come do your share like a man.

[CHORUS]

There is power, there is power
  In a band of working men
    When they stand
    Hand in hand.
That's a power, that's a power
  That must rule in every land,
    One Industrial Union Grand.

Would you have mansions of gold in the sky,
  And live in a shack
  Away in the back?
Would you have wings up in heaven to fly
  And starve here with rags on your back?

[CHORUS]

If you've had enough of the Blood of the Lamb,
  Then join in the Grand Industrial Band.
If, for a change, you would have eggs and ham,
  Then come do your share like a man.

[CHORUS]

If you like sluggers to beat off your head,
  Then don't organize,
  All unions despise.
If you want nothing before you are dead,
  Shake hands with your boss and look wise.

[CHORUS]

Come all you workers from every land,
  Come join in the Great Industrial Band.
Then we our share of this earth shall demand.
  Come on, do your share like a man.

[CHORUS]

I.W.W. Song, probably J O E H I L L [b.?, d. 1919]

★★★★★★★

Our cities grew and grew. Manhattan and Brooklyn were linked in 1884 by a bridge that was an engineering wonder. Fifty years after its opening, Hart Crane could still sing about it as a symbol of American life. Geronimo, the last of the hostile Indian warriors, was captured by General Miles in 1886, the same year that the Statue of Liberty, by the sculptor Bartholdi, a gift from the French Republic, was dedicated by President Grover Cleveland in New York harbor. We continued to make new myths as gold was discovered in the Klondike and Alaska's frozen mountains became as attractive as California had been in 1849.

Women who up to now had been kept decently quiet or excessively busy in the home, began to make their voices heard on the national scene; not only did they demand the right to vote, some of them insisted on dressing up in Mrs. Amelia Jenks Bloomer's new-fangled pantaloons!

To Brooklyn Bridge
☆

How many dawns, chill from his rippling rest
The seagull's wings shall dip and pivot him,
Shedding white rings of tumult, building high
Over the chained bay waters Liberty—

Then, with inviolate curve, forsake our eyes
As apparitional as sails that cross
Some page of figures to be filed away;
—Till elevators drop us from our day . . .

I think of cinemas, panoramic sleights
With multitudes bent toward some flashing scene
Never disclosed, but hastened to again,
Foretold to other eyes on the same screen;

And Thee, across the harbor, silver-paced
As though the sun took step of thee, yet left
Some motion ever unspent in thy stride,—
Implicitly thy freedom staying thee!

Out of some subway scuttle, cell or loft
A bedlamite speeds to thy parapets,
Tilting there momently, shrill shirt ballooning,
A jest falls from the speechless caravan.

Down Wall, from girder into street noon leaks,
A rip-tooth of the sky's acetylene;
All afternoon the cloud-flown derricks turn . . .
Thy cables breathe the North Atlantic still.

And obscure as that heaven of the Jews,
Thy guerdon . . . Accolade thou dost bestow

Of anonymity time cannot raise:
Vibrant reprieve and pardon thou dost show.

O harp and altar, of the fury fused,
(How could mere toil align thy choiring strings!)
Terrific threshold of the prophet's pledge,
Prayer of Pariah, and the lover's cry,—

Again the traffic lights that skim thy swift
Unfractioned idiom, immaculate sigh of stars,
Beading thy path—condense eternity:
And we have seen night lifted in thine arms.

Under thy shadow by the piers I waited;
Only in darkness is thy shadow clear.
The City's fiery parcels all undone,
Already snow submerges an iron year . . .

O Sleepless as the river under thee,
Vaulting the sea, the prairies' dreaming sod,
Unto us lowliest sometime sweep, descend
And of the curveship lend a myth to God.

HART CRANE [1899-1932]

Geronimo

☆

Beside that tent and under guard
In majesty alone he stands,
As some chained eagle, broken-winged,
With eyes that gleam like smouldering brands,—
A savage face, streaked o'er with paint,
And coal-black hair in unkempt mane,

Thin, cruel lips, set rigidly,—
A red Apache Tamerlane.

As restless as the desert winds,
Yet here he stands like carven stone,
His raven locks by breezes moved
And backward o'er his shoulders blown;
Silent, yet watchful as he waits
Robed in his strange, barbaric guise,
While here and there go searchingly
The cat-like wanderings of his eyes.

The eagle feather on his head,
Is dull with many a bloody stain,
While darkly on his lowering brow
Forever rests the mark of Cain.
Have you but seen a tiger caged
And sullen through his barriers glare?
Mark well his human prototype
The fierce Apache fettered there.

ERNEST MCGAFFEY

The Bartholdi Statue
☆

The land, that, from the rule of kings,
In freeing us, itself made free,
Our Old World Sister, to us brings
Her sculptured Dream of Liberty:

Unlike the shapes of Egypt's sands
Uplifted by the toil-worn slave,
On Freedom's soil with freemen's hands
We rear the symbol free hands gave.

O France, the beautiful! to thee
Once more a debt of love we owe:
In peace beneath thy Colors Three,
We hail a later Rochambeau!

Rise, stately Symbol! holding forth
Thy light and hope to all who sit
In chains and darkness! Belt the earth
With watch-fires from thy torch up-lit!

Reveal the primal mandate still
Which Chaos heard and ceased to be,
Trace on mid-air th' Eternal Will
In signs of fire: "Let man be free!"

Shine far, shine free, a guiding light
To Reason's ways and Virtue's aim,
A lightning-flash the wretch to smite
Who shields his license with thy name!

JOHN GREENLEAF WHITTIER [1807-1892]

The Klondike

☆

Never mind the day we left, or the way the women clung
    to us;
All we need now is the last way they looked at us.
Never mind the twelve men there amid the cheering—
Twelve men or one man, 't will soon be all the same;
For this is what we know: we are five men together,
Five left o' twelve men to find the golden river.

Far we came to find it out, but the place was here for all
    of us;
Far, far we came, and here we have the last of us.
We that were the front men, we that would be early,
We that had the faith, and the triumph in our eyes:
We that had the wrong road, twelve men together,—
Singing when the devil sang to find the golden river.

Say the gleam was not for us, but never say we doubted it;
Say the wrong road was right before we followed it.
We that were the front men, fit for all forage,—

Say that while we dwindle we are front men still;
For this is what we know to-night: we're starving here
    together—
Starving on the wrong road to find the golden river.

Wrong, we say, but wait a little: hear him in the corner
    there;
He knows more than we, and he'll tell us if we listen
    there—
He that fought the snow-sleep less than all the others
Stays awhile yet, and he knows where he stays:
Foot and hand a frozen clout, brain a freezing feather,
Still he's here to talk with us and to the golden river.

"Flow," he says, "and flow along, but you cannot flow away
    from us;
All the world's ice will never keep you far from us;
Every man that heeds your call takes the way that leads
    him—
The one way that's his way, and lives his own life:
Starve or laugh, that game goes on, and on goes the river;
Gold or no, they go their way—twelve men together.

"Twelve," he says, "who sold their shame for a lure you
    call too fair for them—
You that laugh and flow to the same word that urges
    them:
Twelve who left the old town shining in the sunset,
Left the weary street and the small safe days:
Twelve who knew but one way out, wide the way or
    narrow:
Twelve who took the frozen chance and laid their lives on
    yellow.

"Flow by night and flow by day, nor ever once be seen by
    them;
Flow, freeze, and flow, till time shall hide the bones of
    them:
Laugh and wash their names away, leave them all
    forgotten,
Leave the old town to crumble where it sleeps;
Leave it there as they have left it, shining in the valley,—
Leave the town to crumble down and let the women
    marry.

"Twelve of us or five," he says, "we know the night is on
    us now;
Five while we last, and we may as well be thinking now:
Thinking each his own thoughts, knowing, when the light
    comes,
Five left or none left, the game will not be lost.
Crouch or sleep, we go the way, the last way together;
Five or none, the game goes on, and on goes the river.

"For after all that we have done and all that we have
    failed to do,
Life will be life and the world will have its work to do:
Every man who follows us will heed in his own fashion
The calling and the warning and the friends who do not
    know;
Each will hold an icy knife to punish his heart's lover,
And each will go the frozen way to find the golden river."

There you hear him, all he says, and the last we'll ever get
    from him.
Now he wants to sleep, and that will be the best for him.
Let him have his own way—no, you needn't shake him—
Your own turn will come, so let the man sleep,

For this is what we know: we are stalled here together—
Hands and feet and hearts of us, to find the golden river.

And there's a quicker way than sleep? . . . Never mind the
    looks of him:
All he needs now is a finger on the eyes of him.
You there on the left hand, reach a little over—
Shut the stars away, or he'll see them all night:
He'll see them all night and he'll see them all tomorrow,
Crawling down the frozen sky, cold and hard and yellow.

Won't you move an inch or two—to keep the stars away
    from him?
—No, he won't move, and there's no need of asking him.
Never mind the twelve men, never mind the women;
Three while we last, we'll let them all go;
And we'll hold our thoughts north while we starve here
    together,
Looking each his own way to find the golden river.

EDWIN ARLINGTON ROBINSON [1869-1935]

Crinolines and Bloomers
or The Battle Between Monsieur Worth
and Mrs. Bloomer
☆

> *The curtain is drawn to reveal M. Worth in the center of a line
> of showgirls wearing crinolines. He sings:*

My name is Mr. Worth,
I am English by birth
But in Paris they all call me Monsieur Worth

And so I think they ought
For in Paris I was taught
And there's no one quite so wonderful on Earth.
I'm ze ladies' pampered pet,
I invent ze *grande-toilette.*
And if you ever see
What they call ze *dernier cri*
It's entirely due to me.
So don't forget,
For driving in ze Bois
I 'ave something quite unique,
It is worn, comme *toutes les fois,*
By ze Princess Metternich.
It is chic, chic, chic,
For ze *robe de soir* also
'Tis to me you have to go.
Never mind your husband's frown,
Never mind ze little debt—
All ze duchesses in town,
Grandes cocottes and cocodettes,
All the ladies come to me,
Je suis *Tout-Paris.*

> *At the end of this he joins with the girls in a dance. Suddenly through the center curtains bursts a strange figure in bloomers. It is no less than Mrs. Bloomer herself, disgusted with Paris fashions. Monsieur Worth and the girls fall aside and Mrs. Bloomer comes to the middle of the stage and sings: (to the tune of "Dixie")*

I'm Amelia Jenks, but American rumor
Prefers to call me Mrs. Bloomer,
From the land of the great, of the free, of the brave.

I'm tired of the women who are fools of fashion,
Lackeys of love and pawns of passion,
And of she who can be of Paree just a slave.

When I saw those foolish fal-lals
I nearly died,
On all those fine upstanding gals,
I never was so mortified.
For ways so dumb
There's only one solution,
And so I've come
To start a revolution.

M. WORTH:

You're Amelia Jenks? What a piece of humor!
Did I hear you say you're *Mrs.* Bloomer?
What a joke, I'd have thought that you were just a lad,
For you have no skirt and have no *jupon*—
You 'ave got nozzing to sew ze hoop on;
It's too bad you are mad, what a fad, *quelle salade!*

When I saw those things you've got on
J'etais comme mort.
A woman in a *pantalon*,
I zinck I nevaire see before.
These clothes you've got

Are simply no solution.
It's *sans-culottes*
Who start a Revolution.

    MRS. BLOOMER:
I'm Amelia Jenks from across the water,
Liberty's child and Columbia's daughter.
Who are you who presume to create such a scene?

    M. WORTH:
I'm Monsieur Worth and I make ze dresses
For all ze duchesses and princesses,
Mousseline, crepe-de-chine, zibelline, crinoline.

    GIRLS:
To take your female skirts off,
Fie, fie, for shame!

    MRS. BLOOMER
Although the world may jeer and scoff,
I'll wear the trousers all the same.
I'll tell the world
There's only one solution.
My flag's unfurled
To start a revolution.

    *At the end of the song she marches up and down the stage. The
girls fall into step behind her. Each girl as she comes to the mid-
dle of the stage, slips off her skirt to appear in bloomers.*

    *The scene ends with Mrs. Bloomer in the middle of the stage,
the girls marking time on either side of her, M. Worth having
fled in horror. Mrs. Bloomer pulls a flag with the stars and
stripes out of her bloomers and waves it over her head as the
curtain falls.*

    —from *British Television,* 1939

There was a real M. Worth, founder of the fashion house which
bore his name in Paris, but there is no historical basis for an
actual confrontation between him and the crusading Mrs. Amelia
Jenks Bloomer. His remark in the skit about *sans-culottes* refers
to the pantless revolutionaries who achieved the French Revolu-
tion a hundred years before.

THE UNITED STATES
AND A WORLD
AT WAR

IN 1914 A QUARREL between Austria and Serbia began to spread. Russia and Germany, England and France were quickly involved. A major European war had broken out. We read the battle news, took comfort in President Wilson's slogan, Peace With Honor, and wondered if it could last. Vachel Lindsay invoked the shade of Lincoln to consider the state of the world.

By 1917, after the sinking of the liner *Luisitania*, we too were in the war. War had become much more mechanical, much less heroic, and poets saw more dirt in it than glory. War had come to be a bad job that might have to be done but could seldom be upheld as a crusade.

I Have a Rendezvous with Death
☆

I have a rendezvous with Death
At some disputed barricade,
When Spring comes back with rustling shade
And apple-blossoms fill the air—
I have a rendezvous with Death
When Spring brings back blue days and fair.
It may be he shall take my hand
And lead me into his dark land
And close my eyes and quench my breath—
It may be I shall pass him still.
I have a rendezvous with Death
On some scarred slope of battered hill,
When Spring comes round again this year
And the first meadow-flowers appear.

God knows 'twere better to be deep
Pillowed in silk and scented down

Where love throbs out in blissful sleep,
Pulse night to pulse, and breath to breath,
Where hushed awakenings are dear . . .
But I've a rendezvous with Death
At midnight in some flaming town;
When Spring trips north again this year,
And I to my pledged word am true,
I shall not fail that rendezvous.

ALAN SEEGER [1888-1916]

"next to of course god america i
love you land of the pilgrims' and so forth oh
say can you see by the dawn's early my
country 'tis of centuries come and go
and are no more what of it we should worry
in every language even deafanddumb
thy sons acclaim your glorious name by gorry
by jingo by gee by gosh by gum
why talk of beauty what could be more beau-
tiful than these heroic happy dead
who rushed like lions to the roaring slaughter
they did not stop to think they died instead
then shall the voice of liberty be mute?"

He spoke. And drank rapidly a glass of water

e. e. cummings [1894-1962]

Abraham Lincoln Walks at Midnight
☆

(*In Springfield, Illinois*)

It is portentous, and a thing of state
That here at midnight, in our little town
A mourning figure walks, and will not rest,
Near the old court-house pacing up and down,

Or by his homestead, or in shadowed yards
He lingers where his children used to play,
Or through the market, on the well-worn stones
He stalks until the dawn-stars burn away.

A bronzed, lank man! His suit of ancient black,
A famous high top-hat and plain worn shawl
Make him the quaint great figure that men love,
The prairie-lawyer, master of us all.

He cannot sleep upon his hillside now.
He is among us:—as in times before!
And we who toss and lie awake for long
Breathe deep, and start, to see him pass the door.

His head is bowed. He thinks on men and kings.
Yea, when the sick world cries, how can he sleep?
To many peasants fight, they know not why,
Too many homesteads in black terror weep.

The sins of all the war-lords burn his heart.
He sees the dreadnaughts scouring every main.
He carries on his shawl-wrapped shoulders now
The bitterness, the folly and the pain.

He cannot rest until a spirit-dawn
Shall come;—the shining hope of Europe free:
The league of sober folk, the Workers' Earth,
Bringing long peace to Cornland, Alp and Sea.

It breaks his heart that kings must murder still,
That all his hours of travail here for men
Seem yet in vain. And who will bring white peace
That he may sleep upon his hill again?

VACHEL LINDSAY [1879-1931]

it's jolly
odd what pops into
your jolly tête when the
jolly shells begin dropping jolly fast you
hear the rrmp and
then nearerandnearerandNEARER
and before
you can
!
& we're
NOT
(oh—
—i say

that's jolly odd
old thing, jolly
odd, jolly
jolly odd isn't
it jolly odd

e. e. cummings [1894-1962]

A Soldier
☆

He is that fallen lance that lies as hurled,
That lies unlifted now, come dew, come rust,
But still lies pointed as it plowed the dust.
If we who sight along it round the world,
See nothing worthy to have been its mark,
It is because like men we look too near,
Forgetting that as fitted to the sphere,
Our missiles always make too short an arc.
They fall, they rip the grass, they intersect
The curve of earth, and striking, break their own;
They make us cringe for metal-point on stone.
But this we know, the obstacle that checked
And tripped the body, shot the spirit on
Further than target ever showed or shone.

ROBERT FROST [1875-1963]

Hugh Selwyn Mauberley
☆

These fought in any case,
and some believing,
pro domo, in any case . . .

Some quick to arm,
some for adventure,
some from fear of weakness,
some from fear of censure,
some for love of slaughter, in imagination,
learning later . . .
some in fear, learning love of slaughter;

Died some, pro patria,
                    non "dulce" non "et decor" . . .
walked eye-deep in hell
believing in old men's lies, then unbelieving
came home, home to a lie,
home to many deceits,
home to old lies and new infamy;
usury age-old and age-thick
and liars in public places.

Daring as never before, wastage as never before.
Young blood and high blood,
fair cheeks, and fine bodies;
fortitude as never before,
frankness as never before,
disillusions as never told in the old days,
hysterias, trench confessions,
laughter out of dead bellies.

EZRA POUND [1885-   ]

BETWEEN WARS

With the rest of the world we hurried to forget the war in the booming years of the 1920's. We went about our jobs with various degrees of well-being and sometimes with the nervous discomfort of J. V. A. Weaver's *Drug Store.* It was a glittering boom era and a jittery one. The Prohibition experiment failed to check drinking and helped spawn an even more highly organized criminal society, although Americans could look on bootleggers with the dry humor of Don Marquis.

And then the boom dived into black and deep depression, nationwide in factory, farm and seaport, worldwide beyond that. There were darkening clouds on the skies across the sea; a war in Spain, Hitler in Germany, Mussolini in Italy, and in Asia aggression by the Japanese against China. Still, there was beginning to be an end of the worst of the depression at home and there were many people who lived like the superficially happy near-automaton of Kenneth Fearing's *Dirge.*

Drug Store
☆

Pardon me, lady, but I wanta ast you,
For God's sake, stop that tappin'! I'll go nuts,
Plain bug-house if I hear that tap-tap-tap
Much longer!
                    Now I went and used such language,
I got to tell you why. . . . Well, in the first place,
My business is all shot. Now drugs theirselves
Don't pay much, and the extra stuff, like candy,
Cigars and stationery and et cetery,
Don't make their keep. And that damn soda-fountain—
Excuse me, lady, but I just can't help it! . . .

Some day I'm gointa catch the guy I bought it off—
I'm losin' money every day it's here.
And soda-jerkers—now I can't get none
For love or money, so myself I got to
Mess with them malted milks, banana splits,
And slop like that. And just as doggone sure
As I start workin' on some fine prescription,
The kind I love to mix—got to be careful
The weights is hittin' on that perfect balance—
Why, then some fool wants a marshmallow sundae,
And tap-tap-tap-he starts in on the show-case,
And taps and taps till I come runnin' out,
Leavin' the drugs half-done.
                    And that ain't all;
Here's the big trouble—I can't talk good grammar.
People don't think a man that mixes drugs
Can do it right and talk the way I do.
It makes me sick—why have I got to sound
Like a schoolteacher? Why, I know my stuff:
"Registered Pharmacist"—see? I taught myself,

Workin' at night while I was four years clerkin';
And then I took three months down at the U,
And passed a fine exam. But here's the thing:
I quit the public school in seventh grade,
And never paid no attention to my talk.
So it's the way I tell you—they're suspicious
Because I use such slang. I try to stop,
But it's too late now. I found out too late. . . .

I got a dream of what I'll do some day:
I want to quit this drug stuff altogether,
Have a nice office, with a big oak desk,
And sell just real estate. I'd like to bet
I'd make a clean-up at it. It'd be swell,
That office . . .
           But this life is killin' me.

It's the fool question they keep askin' me!
You see that clock there? Well, just on a guess
Three times an hour some silly fish comes in here
And calls me out, and asts me, "Is that right?—
Is your clock right?" Honest to Heaven, lady,
One day I got so sore I took a hammer
And smashed the face in. And it cost twelve dollars
To fix it. But I had peace for a week.
O, gosh, my nerves! . . . But that's the way it is
I'm sorry I spoke so rough about that tappin',
But when I get to sellin' real estate,
They'll be no place where folks can take a coin
And tap, and tap, till I come runnin' out.
That's a man's business! . . .
             If I ever get it. . . .

JOHN V. A. WEAVER [1898-1938]

Recuerdo

☆

We were very tired, we were very merry
We had gone back and forth all night on the ferry.
It was bare and bright, and smelled like a stable—
But we looked into a fire, we leaned across a table,
We lay on a hill-top underneath the moon;
And the whistles kept blowing, and the dawn came soon.

We were very tired, we were very merry—
We had gone back and forth all night on the ferry;
And you ate an apple, and I ate a pear,
From a dozen of each we had bought somewhere;
And the sky went wan, and the wind came cold,
And the sun rose dripping, a bucketful of gold.

We were very tired, we were very merry,
We had gone back and forth all night on the ferry.
We hailed, "Good morrow, mother!" to a shawl-covered
    head,
And bought a morning paper, which neither of us read;
And she wept, "God bless you!" for the apples and pears,
And we gave her all our money but our subway fares.

EDNA ST. VINCENT MILLAY [1892-1950]

Mrs. Swartz

☆

A Ballad of Prohibition

*"WHEELING, W. VA.—Prohibition agents who surprised Mrs. Mike
Swartz of Poggs Run while she was operating a still today, heeded the*

pleas of her nine children and refused to arrest her. Mike Swartz, her husband, is in a Federal prison for robbing a freight car."—NEWS STORY.

The Prohibition agents came
    Unto a cabin door,
Nine angel children played their games
    And romped upon the floor;
The agents laid a burly hand
    On Mother's hair so gray,
For making hootch, you understand,
    And all the Tots did say:

"Oh, do not take our Mother's still
    for she is old and worn,
What will she do if she can't make
    the moonshine from the corn?
O, do not lock our Mother up!
    What will become of we
Without the hootch we learned to drink
    at dear old Mother's knee?"

The Prohibition agents then
    Felt tears fall down their cheek,
At heart they were not wicked men,
    Oh, they were only weak!
And both removed their burly hands
    From Mother's hair so gray;
They felt remorse, you understand,
    And to the Tots did say:

    [CHORUS]

The eldest daughter thanked them then,
    A maid of sweet sixteen,

Who had not often spoke to men,
   She was a little queen.
She smiled at them above her tears,
   So fairy-like and gay,
And said, "I'll thank you all my years,
   Because you just did say:

    [CHORUS]

The youngest agent spoke to her:
  "You look so sweet and pure!
What man would be so low a cur
  As think to you injure?
I offer you on bended knee
  All of my manly love!"
An Angel Voice that sang in glee
  Came to them from Above:

  [CHORUS]

Just then a lusty shout was heard
  Outside the cabin door,
A clean-shaven man with coat all furred
  Came riding in a Ford.
It was their Father who'd escaped
  From jail that very day,
And kneeling down among them prayed
  While all of them did say:

  [CHORUS]

DON MARQUIS [1878-1937]

Down on Roberts' Farm
  ☆

Come, ladies and gentlemen, listen to my song.
I'll sing it to you now, but you might think it wrong.
It might make you mad, but I mean no harm—
It's about the workers on Roberts' Farm.

  It's hard times in the country
  Down on Roberts' Farm.

You move out to Mr. Roberts' Farm,
Plant a big crop o' cotton and a little crop o' corn,
Come around the plans and the plot
Till he gets a chattel mortgage on everything you got.

It's hard times in the country
Down on Roberts' Farm.

．　．　．　．　．　．　．　．　．　．

I moved down to Mr. Roberts' Farm.
I worked on the dairy, I worked on the farm.
I milked old Brindle and she had one horn.
It's hell to be a renter down on Roberts' Farm.

It's hard times in the country
Down on Roberts' Farm.

．　．　．　．　．　．　．　．　．　．

Roberts' renters, they go downtown,
With their hands in their pockets and their heads
      hung down.
They go in the store and the merchant will say:
"Your mortgage is due and I'm lookin' for my pay."

It's hard times in the country
Down on Roberts' Farm.

Went down to my pocket with a tremblin' hand,
"I can't pay you all, but I'll do what I can."
The merchant jumped to the telephone call:
"I'm goin' to put you in jail, if I don't get it all!"

It's hard times in the country
Down on Roberts' Farm.

Mr. Paul Roberts with a big Overland,
He's a little tough-luck kid don't give a damn.
He'll run you in the mud like a train on a track.
He'll haul you to the mountain, but he won't haul you
    back.

It's hard times in the country
Down on Roberts' Farm.

CLAUDE REEVES [c. 1935]

Share-cropping in theory allowed a renter to work land and live
off part of the yield he split with the land-owner. Too often, and
especially during the worst of the depression years, unscrupulous
land-owners managed to cozen their renters into a degree of
debt that turned them into near-slaves. Mr. Paul Roberts' Over-
land was an automobile of the period, no longer in production;
like share-cropping (but more honorably), a depression casualty.

What Shall We Do for the Striking Seamen?
☆

What shall we do for the striking seamen?
What shall we do for the striking seamen?
What shall we do for the striking seamen?
    Help them win their battle!

Oh! Ho! And all together!
Oh! Ho! And all together!
Oh! Ho! And all together!
    Help them win their battle!

Turn in food for the striking seamen.
Turn in food for the striking seamen.

Turn in food for the striking seamen.
  Help them win their battle!

Oh! Ho! And all together, etc.

Share our homes with the striking seamen.
Share our homes with the striking seamen.
Share our homes with the striking seamen.
  Help them win their battle!

Oh! Ho! And all together, etc.

March on the line for the striking seamen!
March on the line for the striking seamen!
March on the line for the striking seamen!
  Help them win their battle!

Oh! Ho! And all together!
Oh! Ho! And all together!
Oh! Ho! And all together!
  Help them win their battle!

> The familiar chanty rhythm of "What Shall We Do for the Drunken Sailor" has been used to turn a traditional work-song into a chant of protest.

Dirge
☆

1-2-3 was the number he played but to-day the number
  came 3-2-1;
bought his Carbide at 30 and it went to 29; had the
  favourite at Bowie but the track was slow—

O, executive type, would you like to drive a floating power,
knee-action, silk-upholstered six? Wed a Hollywood
star? Shoot the course in 58? Draw to the ace, king,
jack?
O, fellow with a will who won't take no, watch out for
three cigarettes on the same, single match; O,
democratic voter born in August under Mars, beware
of liquidated rails—

Denouement to denouement, he took a personal pride in
the certain, certain way he lived his own, private life,
but nevertheless, they shut off his gas; nevertheless,
the bank foreclosed; nevertheless, the landlord called;
nevertheless, the radio broke,

And twelve o'clock arrived just once too often, just the
same he wore one grey tweed suit, bought one straw
hat, drank one straight Scotch, walked one short step,
took one long look, drew one deep breath, just one too
many,

And wow he died as wow he lived, going whop to the
office and blooie home to sleep and biff got married
and bam had children and oof got fired, zowie did he
live and zowie did he die,

With who the hell are you at the corner of his casket, and
where the hell we going on the right hand silver knob,
and who the hell cares walking second from the end
with an American Beauty wreath from why the hell
not,

Very much missed by the circulation staff of the New York
Evening Post; deeply, deeply mourned by the B.M.T.,

Wham, Mr. Roosevelt; pow, Sears Roebuck; awk, big
  dipper; bob, summer rain; bong, Mr. bong Mr. bong,
  Mr. bong.

KENNETH FEARING [1902-1961]

WORLD WAR II
AND AFTER

THE CLOUDS gathered together and suddenly there was war again in Europe, war more unreal, more mechanical, slower and dirtier than even the last one. We read the battle news again and wondered again.

We hoped against experience that we could stay out of war, but on December 7, 1941, Japanese planes struck at our base at Pearl Harbor, Hawaii, and we were in a World War that this time truly covered the whole world.

World War II's verse followed the First World War's pattern with personal feelings and acute observation taking the place of the heroic stanzas of the past. We sang of war in the air as well as on the ground, of strange new necessities like blackouts, and we hoped again that this war might be the last one.

Camptown
☆

The streets that slept all afternoon in sun
Waken in neon. Now the buses run
In brightest bugeyes from the darkening camp,
Sway on the local traffic, stamp
Frantic brakes heart-inches from collision,
Bumble a new start, and by long revision
Kiss the stone curbs on which the doors are thrown
Wide, wider—and a drumbeat stirs the town.

Yellow skirt girl will you kiss me tonight
From the river farm to the marquis light,
The mail order catalogue home on the shelf
Modeling the dream of your dreamy self,
Red blouse girl on the spinning year
Blue hat, bright hat, here, here, here,
The kiss of your pose across your fright
And the kiss of the wish we wish tonight.

Whirling on the sidewalk, eddying the street,
Dammed where the juke box tom-toms beat.
Yellow skirt girl the dust I've seen,
Red blouse girl the days between
Breast and breast of a night in town,
The bugles tears and the light turned down,
And the talk of you, the talk of you,
The silence and the center of the tents—of you.

Yellow skirt, red blouse, blue hat, bright,
Quilt the covers of your heart tonight.
Swallow me down the music's beat,
Follow my heart and follow my feet.
Follow my days to the weeks between

Where the land is the dust of a hot machine.
Follow where the drums and the brass run down
For the same dream brought us both to town.

Over the river and the running ranges,
Over the moon—While the record changes:
Last minute boogie, now, now, now,
In the park, in the doorway, no matter how—
Follow, follow, till the neons drop,
One by one the flash-signs stop,
One by one it's over and done—
And we're late and lost unless we run.

                                        JOHN CIARDI [1916-   ]

> Marquis lights would seem to refer to movie-house signs; the
> more familiar spelling—marquee.

Memorial to the Great Big Beautiful Self-Sacrificing Advertisers
   ☆

Look, we don't give a hoot if Zippo-Fasteners have gone
     to war
(millions of us, by some strange coincidence, have done
     the same thing):
and it isn't likely to break our hearts if we can't buy one
     today
or tomorrow or whenever it was we were going to buy a
     Zippo, or whatever for—
We believe Life will somehow go on.

And it doesn't matter too terribly much to us in the front
     lines

if Old Cask whiskey is rationed: not to us for whom it has
   been
rationed so thinly that we haven't seen a label in eleven
   months.
Cease worrying us with you nobility: yours is no national
   disaster,
your apologies are beginning to wear thin.

If your magazine is late—
If you can't reserve a lower berth—
If you can't purchase Durafilm—
If your long-distance call is held up—
So what! Cease the (advt.) threnody:
Nobody's going to die because of this.

War in itself is a vulgarity; it should not be an excuse for
   advertisers
to parade their enormous sacrifice behind a thin screen of
   bond pleas,
of shallow regrets, of four-color-process hypocrisy. We can
   stand only so much
of a hard-luck story; then we begin to wonder about your
   sincerity.
Isn't the government paying you for your product? Okay,
   then—pipe down!
We're being paid too for our blood and our legs and our
   eyes and our arms,
and we're not making a full-page song-and-dance about it.

The pattern is all too familiar: bright shells burst on the
   page;
tanks rear and planes crash (the artist's conception of
   war)
in the midst of well-ordered disaster. Not so much blood
   and filth,

of course, as to offend good taste—oh, the immaculate
    conception of war—
and then the sob-line about no cigarette lighters today, no
    bath scales
no aluminum lids for your poor, poor desolate cleansing
    cream:
some day somebody will fracture an arm thus publicly
    waving a flag.

The woman in Saginaw who reads the telegram of regret
from the government, for her only son—
and the lad on the cruiser who's just seen his pal
blown to hell in a loud flash—
they too feel the impact of war, but they can't put their
    grief
in a $5,000 lithograph and ask you to cry with them.
There is a dignity in silence.

FREDRICK EBRIGHT [1912-   ]

During the war there was much ado in four-color advertising
displays about sacrifices on the home front, civilian hardships
and the wonderful ways in which industry was serving the war
effort. Most such claims were reasonable enough, but to the sol-
dier serving overseas they were mawkish, overdone and even in-
sulting as Mr. Ebright's verse accurately records.

plato told
him: he couldn't
believe it (jesus

told him; he
wouldn't believe
it) lao

tsze
certainly told
him, and general
(yes

mam)
sherman;
and even
(believe it
or

not) you
told him: i told
him; we told him
(he didn't believe it, **no**

sir) it took
a nipponized bit of
the old sixth

avenue
el; in the top of his head: to tell

him

                           e. e. cummings [1894-1962]

"nipponized bit of the old sixth avenue el" refers to a popular piece of folklore. It was believed that the scrap metal from New York's demolished elevated railroad had been sold to the Japanese who had made from it the very shells which were killing American GIs in the war. Actually, some Sixth Avenue El scrap probably was sold to Japan, but its use would have been for armor plate, for ship and tank construction rather than for shrapnel.

Kilroy
☆

I

Also Ulysses once—that other war.
(Is it because we find his scrawl
Today on every privy door
That we forget his ancient rôle?)
Also was there—he did it for the wages—
When a Cathay-drunk Genoese set sail.
Whenever "longen folk to goon on pilgrimages,"
Kilroy is there;
  he tells The Miller's Tale.

II

At times he seems a paranoiac king
Who stamps his crest on walls and says, "My own!"
But in the end he fades like a lost tune,
Tossed here and there, whom all the breezes sing.
"Kilroy was here"; these words sound wanly gay.
Haughty yet tired with long marching.
He is Orestes—guilty of what crime?—
For whom the Furies still are searching;
When they arrive, they find their prey
(Leaving his name to mock them) went away.
Sometimes he does not flee from them in time:
"Kilroy was—" (*With his blood a dying man wrote half
The phrase out in Bataan.*)

III

Kilroy, beware. "HOME" is the final trap
That lurks for you in many a wily shape:
In pipe-and-slippers plus a Loyal Hound
Or fooling around, just fooling around.
Kind to the old (their warm Penelope)
But fierce to boys,
    thus "home" becomes that sea,
Horribly disguised, where you were always drowned,—
(How could suburban Crete condone
The yarns you would have V-mailed from the sun?)—
And folksy fishes sip Icarian tea.

*One stab of hopeless wings imprinted your
Exultant Kilroy-signature
Upon sheer sky for the world to stare:
"I was there! I was there! I was there!"*

IV

God is like Kilroy; He, too, sees it all;
That's how He knows of every sparrow's fall;

That's why we prayed each time the tightropes cracked
On which our loveliest clowns contrived their act.
The G. I. Faustus who was everywhere
Strolled home again. "What was it like outside?"
Asked Can't, with his good neighbors Ought and But
And pale Perhaps and grave-eyed Better Not;
For "Kilroy" means: the world is very wide.
He was there, he was there, he was there!

And in the suburbs Can't sat down and cried.

PETER VIERECK [1916-   ]

Kilroy was a spontaneous folk-lore creation of World War II.
Somewhere, someone scrawled the mystic phrase "Kilroy was
here" on some far-from-home artifact, and the catch-phrase
caught, ineradicably. "Kilroy was here" followed American GIs
across Europe and through the Pacific and Kilroy became a
synonym for the American soldier overseas.

Elegy for a Dead Soldier
☆

I

A white sheet on the tail-gate of a truck
Becomes an altar; two small candlesticks
Sputter at each side of the crucifix
Laid round with flowers brighter than the blood,
Red as the red of our apocalypse,
Hibiscus that a marching man will pluck
To stick into his rifle or his hat,
And great blue morning-glories pale as lips
That shall no longer taste or kiss or swear.
The wind begins a low magnificat,
The chaplain chats, the palm trees swirl their hair,
The columns come together through the mud.

XI

The time to mourn is short that best becomes
The military dead. We lift and fold the flag,
Lay bare the coffin with its written tag,
And march away. Behind, four others wait
To lift the box, the heaviest of loads.
The anesthetic afternoon benumbs,
Sickens our senses, forces back our talk.
We know that others on tomorrow's roads
Will fall, ourselves perhaps, the man beside,
Over the world the threatened, all who walk:
And could we mark the grave of him who died
We would write this beneath his name and date:

EPITAPH

Underneath this wooden cross there lies
A Christian killed in battle. You who read,
Remember that this stranger died in pain;
And passing here, if you can lift your eyes
Upon a peace kept by a human creed,
Know that one soldier has not died in vain.

New Guinea, 1944   KARL SHAPIRO [1913-   ]

Christmas Eve under Hooker's Statue
☆

Tonight a blackout. Twenty years ago
I hung my stocking on the tree, and hell's
Serpent entwined the apple in the toe
To sting the child with knowledge. Hooker's heels
Kicking at nothing in the shifting snow,
A cannon and a cairn of cannon balls
Rusting before the blackened Statehouse, know

How the long horn of plenty broke like glass
In Hooker's gauntlets. Once I came from Mass;

Now storm-clouds shelter Christmas, once again
Mars meets his fruitless star with open arms,
His heavy saber flashes with the rime,
The war-god's bronzed and empty forehead forms
Anonymous machinery from raw men;
The cannon on the Common cannot stun
The blundering butcher as he rides on Time—
The barrel clinks with holly. I am cold:
I ask for bread, my father gives me mould;

His stocking is full of stones. Santa in red
Is crowned with wizened berries. Man of war,
Where is the summer's garden? In its bed
The ancient speckled serpent will appear,
And black-eyed Susan with her frizzled head.
When Chancellorsville mowed down the volunteer,
"All wars are boyish," Herman Melville said;
But we are old, our fields are running wild:
Till Christ again turn wanderer and child.

ROBERT LOWELL [1917-   ]

V-Letter
☆

I love you first because your face is fair,
   Because your eyes Jewish and blue,
Set sweetly with the touch of foreignness
Above the cheekbones, stare rather than dream.
Often your countenance recalls a boy
   Blue-eyed and small, whose silent mischief
Tortured his parents and compelled my hate
   To wish his ugly death.
Because of this reminder, my soul's trouble,
And for your face, so often beautiful,
   I love you, wish you life.

I love you first because you wait, because
   For your own sake, I cannot write
Beyond these words. I love you for these words
That sting and creep like insects and leave filth.
I love you for the poverty you cry
   And I bend down with tears of steel
That melt your hand like wax, not for this war
   The droplets shattering
Those candle-glowing fingers of my joy,
But for your name of agony, my love,
   That cakes my mouth with salt.

And all your imperfections and perfections
   And all your magnitude of grace
And all this love explained and unexplained
Is just a breath. I see you woman-size
And this looms larger and more goddess-like
   Than silver goddesses on screens.
I see you in the ugliness of light,
   Yet you are beautiful,

And in the dark of absence your full length
Is such as meets my body to the full
    Though I am starved and huge.

You turn me from these days as from a scene
    Out of an open window far
Where lies the foreign city and the war.
You are my home and in your spacious love
I dream to march as under flaring flags
    Until the door is gently shut.
Give me the tearless lesson of your pride,
    Teach me to live and die
As one deserving anonymity,
The mere devotion of a house to keep
    A woman and a man.

Give me the free and poor inheritance
    Of our own kind, not furniture
Of education, nor the prophet's pose,
The general cause of words, the hero's stance,
The ambitious incommensurable with flesh,
    But the drab makings of a room
Where sometimes in the afternoon of thought
    The brief and blinding flash
May light the enormous chambers of your will
And show the gracious Parthenon that time
    Is ever measured by.

As groceries in a pantry gleam and smile
    Because they are important weights
Bought with the metal minutes of your pay,
So do these hours stand in solid rows,
The dowry for a use in common life.
    I love you first because your years
Lead to my matter-of-fact and simple death

Or to our open marriage,
And I pray nothing for my safety back,
Not even luck, because our love is whole
    Whether I live or fail.

KARL SHAPIRO [1913-   ]

V-mail stood for a process of photographic reproduction by
which letters to soldiers overseas were transmitted at a rate less
than the usual postage. It was, in its way, a convenience, but
the arrival of a V-letter, something like a small, smudged photo-
stat of actual sentiment and communication could never equal
the excitement of a "real" letter.

For the One Who Would Take Man's Life in His Hands
☆

Tiger Christ unsheathed his sword,
Threw it down, became a lamb.
Swift spat upon the species, but
Took two women to his heart.
Samson who was strong as death
Paid his strength to kiss a slut.
Othello that stiff warrior
Was broken by a woman's heart.
Troy burned for a sea-tax, also for
Possession of a charming whore.
What do all examples show?
What must the finished murderer know?

You cannot sit on bayonets,
Nor can you eat among the dead.
When all are killed, you are alone,
A vacuum comes where hate has fed.

Murder's fruit is silent stone,
The gun increases poverty.
With what do these examples shine?
The soldier turned to girls and wine.
Love is the tact of every good,
The only warmth, the only peace.

"What have I said?" asked Socrates,
"Affirmed extremes, cried yes and no,
Taken all parts, denied myself,
Praised the caress, extolled the blow,
Soldier and lover quite deranged
Until their motions are exchanged.
—What do all examples show?
What can any actor know?
The contradiction in every act,
The infinite task of the human heart."

DELMORE SCHWARTZ [1913-   ]

Not every American embraced the fact of war wholeheartedly.
In World War II (as in World War I) there were men who re-
fused to serve or even to register for the draft for reasons of
religious dissent or personal philosophy. We had come a small
step forward in tolerance, and although many CO's (for Con-
scientious Objector) were reviled and persecuted a few were
respected for the honesty and durability of their convictions.

Christmas 1945
☆

This is the promise that hangs on the tree
Next to the brightly colored ball, reflecting
Light with the tinsel, heartening children
To reach out their hands to grasp it—
"Peace, and good will."

"Why can't I reach it?" the child asks.
"Why do we never reach it?" the child grown older
Asks after the mud of France and Buna,
After the corpses that fertilized the Huertgen Forest
Or flaked off flesh to leave white bones on Iwo.

Why can't we reach it, if we grow as men?
The tinsel ornaments that teased the child,
The child can reach with years, but Man
Grows older, wiser, more proficient in play and work,
To have his hopes elude him still.

The simplest thing we fought for was this peace,
And still our world wheels small among the stars,
A sphere in chaos, split by sound of guns,
Giving off vapor of decaying dead, confused
And irritable with argument and hate.

This peace we soldiers know as victory
Must be more than the end of some years' war,
Must be more than an iridescent trimming
Packed up in paper when the tree is down
To be forgotten for another twelvemonth.

Peace to be kept must live, to live must have
Good will toward men to nourish every breath
And moment of its being. We, the men
Who fought well, fell, suffered or stayed at home,
Must speak for all men everywhere.

Our hopes can't reconvert like planes or tanks,
Be scrapped like guns or uniforms.
Our hopes must live, our Christmas be
More than mere thanks for home or dreams of home,
But resolution for the future.

There are good Christmas words said on this day:
"Peace and good will." They have been words
Too long; they must be acts and feeling now,
And full of meaning. They must be taken off the tree
To make a battle cry for waging peace.

AL HINE [1915-   ]

★★★★★★★

There was relief at the war's end and still as much hope
as disillusionment. We and the world rushed to catch up
with the years we had lost. There were new newnesses
and changes that had only been dreams before. Women
had had the vote so long that Miss McGinley's *Old Feminist* could die unhappy for lack of conflict. But there
was conflict in many another area. The industrial unions
that had been a dream fantasy to the Wobblies had become a fact during the depression, but there were still
labor and employment problems, especially over the
question of retirement and pensions. The Civil War
had been fought a hundred years ago, but the question
of equal rights for the Negro was still unsettled and a
bitter thorn to millions who happened not to have been
born with fair complexions. Like labor and other social
crusaders before them, they borrowed hymn tunes for
the new words of their protest: We Shall Overcome.

Our problems and disaffections could not slow the
pace of invention and accomplishment. Men looked at
the stars with wonder still, but also with the calculated
knowledge that someday we might reach them.

Redeployment
☆

They say the war is over. But water still
Comes bloody from the taps, and my pet cat
In his disorder vomits worms which crawl
Swiftly away. Maybe they leave the house.
These worms are white, and flecked with the cat's
   blood.

The war may be over. I know a man
Who keeps a pleasant souvenir, he keeps
A soldier's dead blue eyeballs that he found
Somewhere—hard as chalk, and blue as slate.
He clicks them in his pocket while he talks.

And now there are cockroaches in the house,
They get slightly drunk on DDT,
Are fast, hard, shifty—can be drowned but not
Without you hold them under quite some time.
People say the Mexican kind can fly.

The end of the war. I took it quietly
Enough. I tried to wash the dirt out of
My hair and from under my fingernails,
I dressed in clean white clothes and went to bed.
I heard the dust falling between the walls.

HOWARD NEMEROV [1920-   ]

Unlike Melville's *Returning Veteran*, the demobilized GI of
World War II had few green valleys to come back to and per-
haps even more than earlier veterans he carried with him still
the soul-deep scars of the evil and destruction he had survived.
No matter how successful the adjustment to peace and civilian
existence, there were ugly images that would haunt many rede-
ployed soldiers all their lives.

Progress
☆

They'll soon be flying to Mars, I hear—
But how do you open a bottle of beer?

A flash will take you from Nome to New York—
But how the hell do you pull a cork?

They'll rocketeer you to Hibernia—
But open a window and get a hernia.

They've stripped space from the widow'd blue—
But where is the lace that fits a shoe?

Where is the key that fits a lock?
Where is the garter that holds a sock?

They'll hop to the moon and skip to the stars,
But what'll stay put are the lids on jars.

This mighty telescope looks far,
But finds no place to park a car.

The world crackles with cosmic minds
Tangled up in Venetian blinds.

One day they'll resurrect the dead,
Who'll die again of colds in the head.

SAMUEL HOFFENSTEIN [1890-1947]

The Silent Generation
☆

When Hitler was the Devil
He did as he had sworn
With such enthusiasm
That even, donnerwetter,
The Germans say, "Far better
Had he been never born!"

It was my generation
That put the Devil down
With great enthusiasm.
But now our occupation
Is gone. Our education
Is wasted on the town.

We lack enthusiasm.
Life seems a mystery;
It's like the play a lady
Told me about: "It's not . . .
It doesn't have a plot,"
She said, "It's history."

LOUIS SIMPSON [1923-   ]

A Poem to Delight My Friends Who Laugh at Science-Fiction
☆

That was the year
the small birds in their frail and delicate battalions
committed suicide against the Empire State,
having in some never-explained manner,
lost their aerial radar, or ignored it.

That was the year
men and women everywhere stopped dying natural deaths.
The aged, facing sleep, took poison;
the infant, facing life, died with the mother in childbirth;
and the whole wild remainder of the population,
despairing but deliberate, crashed in auto accidents
on roads as clear and uncluttered as ponds.

That was the year every ship on every ocean,
every lake, harbor, river, vanished without trace;
and even ships docked at quays
turned over like wounded animals, harpooned whales, or
    Normandies.
Yes, and the civilian transcontinental planes
found, like the war-planes, the sky-lanes crowded
and, praising Icarus, plunged to earth in flames.

Many, mild stay-at-homes, slipped in bathtubs,
others, congenital indoors-men, descending stairs,
and some, irrepressible roisterers, playing musical chairs.
Tots fell from scooter cars and tricycles
and casual passersby were stabbed by falling icicles.

Alas, what carnage! It was reported
that even bicarb and aspirin turned fatal,
and seconal too, to those with mild headaches,
whose stomachs were slightly acid, or who found they
    could not sleep.
All lovers died in bed, as all seafarers on the deep.

Till finally the only people left alive
were the soldiers sullenly spread on battlefields
among the shell-pocked hills and the charred trees.
Thus, even the indispensable wars died of ennui.

But not the expendable conscripts: they remained as
    always.
However, since no transport was available anywhere,
and home, in any case, was dead, and bare,
the soldiers wandered eternally
in their dazed, early-Chirico landscapes,
like drunken stars in their shrinking orbits
round and round and round and round.

And (since I too died in the world-wide suicide)
they may still, for all I know, be there.
Like forsaken chessmen abandoned by paralyzed players,
they may still be there,
may still be there.

EDWIN ROLFE [1909-   ]

The Old Feminist
  ☆

Snugly upon the equal heights
  Enthroned at last where she belongs,
She takes no pleasure in her Rights
  Who so enjoyed her Wrongs.

PHYLLIS MCGINLEY [1905-   ]

Too Old to Work
  ☆

You work in the factory all of your life,
  Try to provide for your kids and your wife.

When you're too old to produce any more,
  They hand you your hat and they show you the
    door.

  [CHORUS]

Too old to work, too old to work,
When you're too old to work and you're too young to die,
Who will take care of you, how'll you get by
When you're too old to work and you're too young to die?

You don't ask for favors when your life is through;
You've got a right to what's coming to you.
Your boss gets a pension when he gets too old.
You helped him retire and you're out in the cold.

  [CHORUS]

They put horses to pasture, they feed 'em on hay,
Even machines get retired some day.
The bosses get pensions when their days are through,
Fat pensions for them, and nothing for you.

[CHORUS]

There's no easy answer, there's no easy cure.
Dreaming won't change it, that's one thing for sure.
But fighting together we'll get there some day,
And when we get there, you will no longer say:

[CHORUS]

Too old to work, too old to work,
When you're too old to work and you're too young to die,
Who will take care of you, how'll you get by
When you're too old to work and you're too young to die?

JOE GLAZER [c. 1950]

We Shall Overcome
☆

We shall overcome,
We shall overcome,
We shall overcome some day.

[CHORUS]

*Oh, deep in my heart
I know that I do believe
We shall overcome some day.*

We shall all be free,
We shall all be free,
We shall all be free some day.

[CHORUS]

We shall walk in peace,
We shall walk in peace,
We shall walk in peace some day.

[CHORUS]

We shall live in peace,
We shall live in peace,
We shall live in peace some day.

[CHORUS]

We shall brothers be,
We shall brothers be,
We shall brothers be some day.

[CHORUS]

Truth shall overcome,
Truth shall overcome,
Truth shall overcome some day.

[CHORUS]

Love shall conquer all,
Love shall conquer all,
Love shall conquer all some day.

[CHORUS]

We'll walk hand in hand,
We'll walk hand in hand,
We'll walk hand in hand some day.

[CHORUS]

This simple and repetitive chant sung in deep sincerity by hundreds and sometimes thousands of Negroes protesting lack of equal rights dramatized their problem to fellow Americans and stood proof against the fire hoses and police dogs of their opponents.

HISTORY IS

ANY OF US who were still naïve enough to believe that History was something entombed in a book ✓ suffered a brutal and direct educational assault November 22, 1963.

The assassination of President John F. Kennedy had all the hideous benefits of our total mass communication. No longer was it possible to wait for news, to have it served to us partially arranged on paper. Minutes after the first confused bulletins, all radio and television brought a nation to Dallas, Texas, to the hospital where the President's body lay, to the churning, self-questioning crowds there and in every city. Suddenly we were all part of a shattering event and most of us, glued to television or radio, remained part of it through the days that followed, up to and past the actual funeral in Washington. It is certain that no major historical event ever imprinted itself so completely on a whole nation and indeed on a listening and watching world.

Channel U.S.A.—Live
☆

We were all passengers in that motorcade,
caught in the dust of a far street
and the stars of flags blown, as the car moved,
bubble-top down, brown hair tossed
above a face familiar as our own.

At home in easy chairs, turning a dial
to bring the image close—the smile, the wave,
the harps of motorcycles and of cheers—
we were, in spite of miles or parties, there;
and ride there still, the underpass ahead,
a building's shadow falling like a tomb
across the narrowing street, the dust, this room
in California-Iowa-Maine,
                the rifle ready, aimed.

Most screens are black and white,
and blood seems only a darker stain.
The carpet's pastel color stays the same,
sofas unblotched. But one fabric turned red
where his torn head had lain.

He campaigned on crutches once;
once scratched a message on a savage coast,
swam more than once through pain,
rescued lost comrades, fought the foam
of inactivity in high, white beds,
worked toward action, wrote,
replaced a brother whom we never knew,
climbed up from foreign fields and died at home
in a loud street where a rifle leaned
its long, blue beak,
                ready and aimed.

A wreath lies where the bullet stopped.
A continent beyond, a live torch burns,
and we, by limousine and plane and jeep,
ride in the flickering caravan,
still caught on an unsteady screen
where westerns blast and haunt our sleep,
making each day the long commute
out of the muck of every street
toward a reviving flame.

We all were passengers, and are,
driving and driven through the sweep
of shadows, sunlight, flags, and love—
but one of us stood up and faced
                the rifle that is always aimed,
and left the image that we keep.

          ADRIEN STOUTENBURG [1916-   ]

★★★★★★★

We bound up our hearts and, at good moments, were able to smile at ourselves with affection for our blemishes along with our virtues.

Star-Spangled Ode
☆
(*For patriotic occasions*)

My country, 'tis to thee and all thy ways
I lift my harp in praise.
Land of tall forests, hills, lakes, seas, and valleys

Of balmy climes and climates somewhat horrider;
Land of Vermont and Maine and also Florider;
Haven to heroes from oppression fleeting
(Viz: Kosciusko, Thomas Mann, and Erike);
Country of Canyons, corn, and central heating,
    Of thee I sing, America!

While statesmen fume and bicker in thy name,
    Thunder upon the Left or damn the Tories,
My task shall be, unblushing, to proclaim
    Thy singular, matchless, and immoderate glories.

    Hail, Columbia, happy spot,
    Gem of a double ocean.
    Here I, embattled patriot,
    Publish my stout devotion.

Hail birthplace of my Gramp.
    Hail customs, monuments, cities, paths, and byways;
Each garden, farm, park, house, and tourist camp,
    And every trailer on your teeming highways.
Hail, land that loved the French and fought the Hessian,
    That dreamed of unearned riches, like Aladdin;
Place of the Uplift, and the graphed Recession,
    Charlie McCarthy, and Bernarr Macfadden!

That in your ample bosom can enclose
Pikes Peak and Billy Rose,
New England lilacs fragrant where you pass,
And the gold poppy in the Western grass.

For good or ill, this is my chosen nation,
    Home of Joe Louis and the D.A.R.,
Fairs, floods, the Federal Investigation,
    And the used car;

Cape Cod, the Coca-Cola, Mount Rainier,
   The Swanee River and the River Bronx,
The Dies Committee and the roasting ear,
   And Scottish songs in swing time at the On'x;
Of rocking chairs on country porches rocking,
And the slim leg in the superlative stocking.

All these do I rejoice in with rejoicing;
   Jones Beach, blueberry pie, and mocking birds,
And Mrs. Doctor Mayo, sweetly voicing
   American Motherhood's authentic words;
And footballs in October attitudes,
And Automats, and packaged breakfast foods.
Now more and evermore
Dear to my heart is this, my native shore,
Where Liberty lingers still, and even Hope
Unvanquished dwells;
Where dentists ply their trade, and there is soap—
Soap, and hot waters steaming, in hotels.
Where none so humble or his lot so low
But in his house there blares the Radio.

   O, beautiful for spacious skies
      And waving fields of grain,
   For everything a buyer buys
      Embalmed in Cellophane.
   America, America,
      I call each prospect good,
   From Maryland
   To the Goldwyn strand
      Of shining Hollywood.

   What do we lack that other nations boast of?
      What splendor or what plague?
   Unanimous Italy may make the most of

Her Duce. We have Hague.
As favorably our plains and mountains size up;
  Our suns are brighter and our snows as chill,
And more profusely do our billboards rise up
  On every templed hill.
And if, beneath the tread of iron heels,
Our earth less sickly reels,
  Where are the armies valianter than these—
Our troops of marching boys assembling yet,
Lads without uniform or bayonet,
  Who come to grips with trees?
And we have Donald Duck and Passamaquoddy,
And more laws than *any*body.

EPILOGUE

Now dies upon my ear
  The eagle screaming and the hollow cheer,
The politician's loud and public tone,
And the La Follette calling to its own.
Only I hear
Above the din, the clamor, the stone-flinging.
Freedom, yet faintly ringing.

And by the dawn's dim light I see you stand,
O indestructible land,
Swaggering still, and binding up your hurts,
  Building your towers, digging impossible ditches;
Your leaders clad in ordinary shirts,
  Your Kennedy clinging to his common britches.
So that I cry, secure within your gates,
O.K., United States.

PHYLLIS MC GINLEY [1905-   ]

Author Index

First Line Index